CHARLES BEDAUX -
DECIPHERING AN ENIGMA

CHARLES BEDAUX -
DECIPHERING AN ENIGMA

SOL BLOOMENKRANZ

iUniverse, Inc.
Bloomington

Charles Bedaux - Deciphering an Enigma

iUniverse books may be ordered through booksellers or by contacting:

iUniverse
1663 Liberty Drive
Bloomington, IN 47403
www.iuniverse.com
1-800-Authors (1-800-288-4677)

ISBN: 978-1-4759-2636-1 (sc)
ISBN: 978-1-4759-2637-8 (ebk)

Printed in the United States of America

iUniverse rev. date: 06/29/2012

CONTENTS

INTRODUCTION

Charles Bedaux was a unique man. In a span of twenty years, he went from being an apprentice pimp on the streets of Montmartre to founder and CEO of the world's largest consulting company. Only in America was this possible—the land of opportunity, where ambitious immigrants were welcomed. But before another twenty years had passed, he committed suicide after being charged for conspiring with an enemy of America. How he went from here to there is the question I have attempted to answer.

Why did I decide to go into the Bedaux story? It gave me the opportunity to review an era in which I had lived and learned of events so cruel to mankind—but also an era so fascinating to professional and amateur historians. I count myself among the latter.

It has been a long time since I've engaged in any kind of serious research. I would never have undertaken this project without the unflagging support and encouragement of my dear wife, Gisela . . . Maria . . . Gertrude. Our youngest grandson, Miles, with his bright, inquisitive questions and comments, has also helped me finish what I hope my readers will find to be a worthwhile effort. Finally, I would also like to thank my editor, Jill Andersen, without whom this never would have come together as a coherent book manuscript.

I must also express my thanks to the archive directors who, upon hearing of my attempt to solve the Bedaux puzzle, brought to my attention many personalities with whom Bedaux associated during the 1930s and 1940s. They shared several eureka moments with me. Thank you, Herr Gregor Pickro of the Bundesarchiv in Koblenz,[1] and Dr. Martin Müller of the Deutsche Bank archive in Frankfurt. In addition, the staff of the Bundesarchiv-Militärarchiv in Freiburg[2] and the Institut für Historische Wissenschaft in Munich were patient and kind in responding to my many queries.

A number of writers have examined the Charles Bedaux story. Most wrote about the contributions he made to the consulting world, for which he gained fame and fortune. Some delved deeper, investigating both the bright side and the dark side of his life. Janet Flanner wrote a three-part series in the September-October 1945 *New Yorker* magazine. Her work encouraged me to dig deeper. Jim Christy wrote a biography about Bedaux highlighting his bright side. Martin Allen wrote the book *Hidden Agenda: How the Duke of Windsor Betrayed the Allies* in 2002, which is about the dark side of the Duke of Windsor and his contact with Bedaux. Charles Glass, in his 2010 work, *Americans in Paris: Life and Death under Nazi Occupation*, was most helpful for his use of American archives.

---

[1]   Or the National Archive in Koblenz, which will hereafter be referred to as BAKoblenz.

[2]   Or the Military Archive in Freiburg, hereafter referred to as MAFreiburg.

My approach to Bedaux was first to engross myself in the literature that has been written about the era and the people he encountered. But most of my story is based on the subsequent information I found in German archives, such as the BAKoblenz, the MAFreiburg, the Deutsche Bank archive, and others.

As Bedaux might have said, it has been an interesting journey.

THE BEGINNING

Charles Eugène Bedaux was born on October 10, 1886, in Charenton, a suburb of Paris. He was one of five children, and his father worked for the French railroad system. His two brothers, Daniel and Gaston, would become engineers, and his sister, Marcelle, would become a seamstress. Young Charles, however, was a school dropout, not completing the equivalent of high school. Atypical for this *petit bourgeois* household, Charles undoubtedly concerned his parents.

What did a young man without a trade or profession do in a village like Charenton? He headed to the big city, Paris, to seek his fortune. At the time, Paris was the third largest city in the Western world, had a population of more than three million, and had hosted the 1900 Olympics. The first Métro line had recently opened and it led to Montmartre—and that is where young Charles went to seek his fortune.

In Montmartre, a district noted for artists and an active nightlife, he was an apprentice to a notorious pimp. But shortly after his mentor was killed in a gang shooting, Bedaux emigrated to the United States. He arrived there on February 14, 1906. By the time he arrived, America had already welcomed about four hundred thousand French emigrants. In fact, America was booming: between 1900 and 1910, eight million immigrants came to the United States. Most of them worked for less money than their native-born brethren, and often took any kind of work. A reasonable wage was twenty dollars a week, and $745 a year was considered a subsistence income.

What was America like at the beginning of the twentieth century? The average life expectancy was forty-seven years, and only 14 percent of homes had a bathtub. The average worker earned between $200 and $400 a year, about twenty-two cents an hour. About 10 percent of adults were illiterate, and 6 percent had graduated from high school.

Like so many others, the young immigrant Charles Bedaux arrived with very little money. He worked a variety of menial jobs, such as washing dishes and construction. When he sold insurance for a short time, he discovered that he was a natural salesman, and outdid most of his competitors.

He traveled west to St. Louis in 1908 and worked as a laborer at Mallinckrodt Chemical. He met and married Blanche de Kressier Allen and had a son, Charles Emile, in 1909.

At the chemical plant, Bedaux moved up the ladder: he was ambitious and eager to learn, and constantly came up with ideas for the company. In 1912 he was able to visit Paris with his young family.

Once back in the United States, Bedaux began working in New York for McKesson-Robbins, a pharmaceutical wholesaler. It was there that he met A. M. Morrini, the Italian industrial engineer. Morrini was visiting the

United States to study worker efficiency measurement methods and scientific management, which Fredrick Taylor had introduced a few years earlier.[3] Morrini needed an interpreter, and hired Bedaux. They traveled the country together to hire a staff of American engineers, and Bedaux accompanied the group of engineers to Europe later that year.

Bedaux stayed in Europe through 1913 and worked for a French consulting company run by Louis Duez. With the outbreak of the war in August 1914, Bedaux enlisted in the French Foreign Legion, but by December he was discharged. According to war department military intelligence division file number 10505-17 national archives, as cited by Martin Allen in *The Hidden Agenda*, Bedaux was discharged from the legion because he suffered from bacillary hemoptysis, a condition that leads to the coughing up of blood. But there is no evidence that Bedaux suffered from this condition; it might have been staged so he could be released from the Legion.

When Bedaux returned to the United States, he and his family settled in Grand Rapids, Michigan. Why Grand Rapids? It was in Grand Rapids that Morrini had made his base and hired Bedaux as his interpreter. But was there a more sinister reason for settling in Grand Rapids? Several companies in Grand Rapids would soon manufacture war material for the Allies, who were engaged in a life-or-death struggle with the Central Powers under the leadership of Germany. And at this time, Germany had agents in place who were engaged in sabotage and espionage, including such

---

[3]   Taylor published *The Principles of Scientific Management* in 1911.

personalities as Franz von Papen and Heinrich Albert. (We will encounter these gentlemen again later in this story.)

Some speculated that Morrini's consulting business was a good cover for an intelligence mission; Italy remained a member of the Central Powers until April 1915, when it entered the war and joined the Allies. Bedaux came under suspicion of being an enemy agent and was investigated by military intelligence. Reports were made, but the war ended before any charges were filed.

In late 1916, Bedaux sent his wife and son to Japan, where they remained until early 1917—a strange and intriguing trip for a young family to make when much of the world was at war. Was there a motive for this, or was it an innocent journey? After all, Charles Bedaux had launched his consulting business and, through his clients, gained access to plant layouts that might have been of interest to a foreign intelligence service. In addition, Bedaux's wife, Blanche, might have been a courier with documents for handover to contacts in Japan. Finally, this roundabout route across the Pacific to Japan would have avoided the British Navy's routine searches of traffic across the Atlantic.

What could have led Bedaux to engage in espionage? Dislike of his former French countrymen? His ego? His audacity? Was he blackmailed? Were his links to the Parisian underworld jeopardizing his consulting business and his chance to become an American citizen?

By 1917, Bedaux became an American citizen, and he and Blanche divorced soon after she returned from Japan.[4] Bedaux quickly married again, this time to Fern Lombard,

---

[4] Blanche soon married a well-to-do, socially prominent American named Albert Laurence Bagnall, whom she had met in Japan.

who was from a prominent family in the Grand Rapids area. This second marriage gave him social stature, which helped his growing business.[5]

---

[5]   Charles Bedaux and Fern Lombard married on July 2, 1917. According to the *Grand Rapids Herald* on July 3, 1917, the couple was driving from Kalamazoo to Grand Rapids when their car's tire was punctured. A clergyman stopped to help and at Bedaux's request, married them on the spot. Bedaux was thirty-one years old and Fern Lombard, the daughter of a lawyer, was twenty-six.

HIS CONSULTING BUSINESS

In 1916, Bedaux had started to do consulting work in Grand Rapids, developing his ideas about increasing worker productivity. His interest in this had been ignited through his work with the Italian engineer A. M. Morrini. Among his clients was Frederic Brearly, a local furniture manufacturer who suggested that Bedaux launch a consulting company and even offered his financial support to do so. Other clients in Grand Rapids included Imperial Furniture Company, Leonard Refrigerator Company, and Valley City Milling Company.

The Bedaux system "standardized all human efforts according to a single unit of measurement, the so-called 'B,' defined as a fraction of a minute of activity plus a fraction of a minute of rest. Workers were expected to achieve a minimum of sixty B per hour and received a bonus for higher B values. In addition, supervisors usually received 25 percent of the bonus as a reward for their role in achieving higher output."[6]

---

[6] Matthias Kipping, "American Management Consulting Companies," 190-220.

It was a modest beginning in Grand Rapids, but in a few short years Bedaux's company became a worldwide enterprise with offices in nineteen countries. It brought him fame and fortune, but also, ultimately, disgrace and death. How did he do it? If any other man had introduced a similar system, it probably would not have flourished.

So let's look at Bedaux. Short in stature, large in ego, clever, with a wonderful French accent that charmed his listeners. A brilliant salesman with considerable personal magnetism, charismatic, an entrepreneur and promoter—all are attributes that describe Charles Bedaux.

Perhaps his clients didn't always understand his explanation of the Bedaux system, but they were interested in getting greater productivity out of their labor force. Investment in new equipment wasn't a high priority at this time, and because his system focused on assembly lines made up of unskilled labor—which were replacing old-fashioned artisans—Bedaux's system seemed ideal.

In 1918, Bedaux moved his seat of operations to Cleveland, Ohio. Cleveland was a much larger market than Grand Rapids, and also the city where John D. Rockefeller launched his mighty oil empire. Could this have been the ambitious Bedaux's motive for moving there?

Cleveland was also where the twenty-five-year-old French engineer Albert Ramond became the sixth employee of the Bedaux company,[7] proving that Bedaux, unlike many

---

[7] Albert Ramond had been in the United States as a naval officer on a mission from the French government in connection with the Allies' war production. A graduate of the prestigious École Nationale Supérieure d'Arts et Métiers, he was destined to play an important role in the life of Bedaux's companies in the United States.

other managers, had the self confidence to hire someone better qualified than he.

Within a short time, Bedaux divided the company into three regional companies with headquarters in New York, Chicago, and San Francisco.[8] From the beginning, however, he had the globe in his sights, and Charles Bedaux International was founded and located in the Chrysler Building in New York City.[9] The overseas operations of early clients such as B. F. Goodrich and Eastman Kodak bridged Bedaux's international expansion. In 1924, Eastman Kodak asked Bedaux to install the "B System" in Great Britain, and by September 1926 he founded Charles E. Bedaux Ltd. in Britain, and its first client was B. F. Goodrich.[10]

In my time researching Bedaux, I had the good fortune to be introduced to John Carney, whose father, Colwell J. Carney, as a young engineering graduate from Cornell University, had joined Bedaux's New York firm in February 1924. The following is based on a memorandum from Colwell J. Carney on his experience with the consultancy:

"A fraction of a minute of work, plus a fraction of a minute of rest, varying in accordance with the nature of the work but always totaling unity"—this was the basic definition of the Bedaux Unit, the "B," and this system would replace the widely used piece-work method of

---

[8] He soon opened additional offices in Boston, Chicago, and Portland. The headquarters for U.S. operations was in New York, at 271 Madison Avenue, and in 1931 it moved to larger quarters at 22 East 40th Street. (*New York Times*, March 25, 1931)

[9] The Bedauxs lived in apartment 12C at 1120 Fifth Avenue.

[10] A 1930 survey by the National Industrial Conference Board showed that the Bedaux System was the most widely used "payment by results" system in the United States.

worker remuneration. According to Carney, it led to "major increases in productivity, increases in hourly earnings, and a reduction in unit costs":

- 40 percent increase in worker productivity
- 20 percent decrease in unit labor costs
- 12.5 percent increase in hourly earnings

With these results, it's understandable why the Bedaux System was so attractive to companies in the 1920s and '30s. In fact, twenty-five major companies in the Rochester, New York, area employed the Bedaux System when Carney was first assigned to this city of five hundred thousand in March 1924.

Young Colwell Carney eventually became extremely successful, earning £25,000 per year and advancing to a management position at Bedaux's London office.

Bedaux consultants were paid according to the following schedule:

Stage of Employment	Salary
Training	$300 per month
First six months	$3.00 per hour*
Second six months	$3.50 per hour*
Third six months (thereafter becoming a resident consultant)	$4.00 per hour*

* These costs were invoiced by Bedaux and paid for by the client.

Bedaux charged clients ten dollars per hour, about twenty times the average hourly earnings for male factory workers at the time.

In Britain, labor unions protested the use of the Bedaux System, viewing it as a threat to employment. The System's aim, after all, was to increase productivity, which could lead to staff reductions. With Britain deep in the Depression in 1929-30 and unemployment reaching 20 percent, company managers suggested that the Bedaux System be modified to better adapt to the country's economic situation. Charles Bedaux refused—and was proven right when the forty-hour workweek was introduced by companies employing the B System.

Bedaux was wise to select outside directors who were well connected and had status in political and commercial circles. He was also interested, however, in men who had social standing in the upper tiers of society. The first chairman of his UK company was Sir Francis Rose (who helped in acquiring the British American Tobacco account), and in Italy his company's first chairman was Giovanni Agnelli of the Fiat family, while the first president was from the Pirelli Tire family.

Bedaux was generous to those who performed well, offering fast promotions and incentive rewards. As an example, Colwell Carney received a bonus of a Rolls Royce in the early 1930s for bringing in clients from South Africa.[11]

---

[11] Carney served in the United States Army Air Corps in the Second World War. He was based in Wright-Patterson Field, where he was involved in aircraft production. After the war, he returned to Britain, where he launched Mead, Carney & Company, a consulting business.

When clients of Bedaux's British office began asking for assistance with their overseas operations, Bedaux International expanded further. In 1932, Imperial Chemical Industries requested a study in South Africa. In 1933, Bedaux worked in Estonia and Latvia on behalf of G. M. Luther Company, which had links to Venesia Ltd., a client in Britain. In 1934, Anglo-Persian Oil Company[12] (now BP) asked for a study of the Abadan refinery, about which we will be hearing about later in the Bedaux saga. The year 1934 also brought about assignments in South Africa and Portugal.

Britain had the most advanced consulting businesses in Europe during the 1930s, and it's safe to say that the Bedaux office in Great Britain was the breeding ground for many of them. Consultants who had learned their trade with Bedaux founded these companies, among others:

- Associated Industrial Ltd.
- PA Consulting Group
- Urwick Orr and Partners
- PE Management Consultants
- Mead, Carney and Partners
- Orr & Boss, Inc.

Bedaux's Italian company was founded in 1927, and Fiat became a client in 1928.[13] The German office opened in 1927 when the American company B. F. Goodrich

---

[12] The company's original name, Anglo-Persian Oil Company, was changed to Anglo-Iranian Oil Company in 1935 when the Shah asked that foreigners use "Iran" rather than "Persia" when referring to his country.

[13] Fiat, employing more than forty thousand in Italy, hired Bedaux to install the Bedaux System. *New York Times,* May 17, 1927.

recommended Bedaux to its German partner, Continental Gummi-Werke. With seventeen engineers staffing the office, it quickly added Deutsche Linoleum-Werke, Vereinigte Glanzstoff, and Rosenthal Porzellan to its client list.

The office in Germany didn't expand as rapidly as the UK office, however, for two reasons. First, worker efficiency agencies were already in place. These included the *Reichskuratorium für Wirtschaftlichkeit* or RKW (National Efficiency Board), which had been founded in 1921 by Carl Friedrich von Siemens and Carl Koetteen to introduce Taylorism and Fordism in Germany, and the *Reichsausschuss für Arbeitszeitermittlung* or REFA (National Committee for Worktime Determination), founded somewhat later.

The second reason, according to professor Paul Erkner's most interesting paper on Continental Gummi-Werke's experience with the B System, was fear that consultants could engage in industrial espionage.[14] When the National Socialists assumed power in 1933, Bedaux's German office was forced to shut down because the Nazis thought it was competing with the German Labor Front headed by Dr. Robert Ley. In the following chapter, we will cover in detail what happened next.

In 1929 a French office was opened, and by 1939 its eighty consultants serviced about 350 clients. Its client list was large because it was the only active consulting business in Europe's three largest markets: the UK, Germany, and France.

---

[14]   Erkner, Paul. *Zeitschrift für Unternehmensgeschichte*, 41, no. 2 (1998): 139-158.

Bedaux opened an office in Amsterdam in 1929 with three major clients: Philips, AKU,[15] and Unilever. With almost no competition, the business boomed and became the launching pad for further international expansion. By the late 1930s, well over one thousand companies in twenty-one countries were using the Bedaux System. This changed the way factories were managed, increasing the importance of the financial director at the cost of the technical director.

This table shows where Bedaux International made its mark:[16]

Country	Year Bedaux Office Opened	Plants Using the Bedaux System	
		1931	1937
United States	1916-1918	52	500
UK	1926	30	336
Germany	1927	21	49
Italy	1927	3	49
France	1929	16	144
Holland	1932-1934	3	39

The Bedaux System had been used in twenty-one countries by 1934. Bedaux had opened offices in Sweden (Stockholm), Australia (Sydney), South Africa (Johannesburg), India (Bombay and Calcutta), Persia (Abadan), and Canada (Toronto). He had more than

---

[15] Now known as Akzo Nobel. It was then known as Algemene Kunstzijde Unie.

[16] Paul Erkner: *"Das Bedaux System: Neue Aspekte der Historischen Rationalisierungs Forschung,"* Zeitschrift für Unternehmungsgeschichte, 1996.

230 clients in the United States and almost 200 clients in Britain.

With the support of Turkey's government, Bedaux opened a company there in 1938 to organize the mining industry and manage the ports. Bedaux met with Mustafa Kemal Atatürk, the founder and first president of the Republic of Turkey, who was in the last months of his life, and received his support. Later that year, Bedaux formed a company in Greece after the dictator Ioannis Metaxis instructed him to reorganize the country's economy to employ the B System.[17]

In 1932, with the international expansion well underway and with his interest in maximizing his personal income by paying minimal taxes, Bedaux founded Bedaux International in Amsterdam.[18] Charles and Fern Bedaux owned 100 percent of Bedaux International. He chose Amsterdam for its low tax rate for foreign-owned enterprises, and soon all client companies were sending their payments to the Amsterdam company. In 1935, Bedaux International moved its offices to the newly constructed Bungehuis, an attractive art nouveau building designed by the renowned Dutch architect A. L. van Gendt, located on Spruisstraat 210. (Bungehuis is now part of the University of Amsterdam).

Some managers had minority shareholdings in Bedaux companies, but Bedaux kept a tight rein on his System. Anyone who left the company was required to sign an agreement prohibiting the use of Bedaux's name and System

---

[17] *New York Times,* August 3, 1938 and October 30, 1938.

[18] He appointed a remarkable woman as manager: Alessandra Ter Hart, whose maiden name was Lubowsky, who was born in Poland in 1902, and who was by now a Dutch or possibly a French national. She was fluent in ten languages and had degrees in engineering, accounting, and law.

and ever mentioning their association with the company. They were also forbidden from working for a Bedaux client for two years. Top-performing managers were rewarded well, with incomes of one hundred thousand dollars or more per year. Based on this and what we know of how Bedaux traveled and lived—deluxe, with a large entourage—his income must have exceeded $1 million per year. He paid minimal taxes.

Bedaux International was a well-organized operation, but there were problems. One was that labor unions felt threatened by what they called the "speed-up system."[19] In 1936, the renowned actor Charlie Chaplin produced and acted in the now-classic film *Modern Times*, a commentary on the industrial world and said to have been inspired by the reaction to the Bedaux System.[20]

In addition, Charles Bedaux was determined to be on the winning side at any cost, and soon developed contacts

---

[19] In September 1934, Kodak Research Laboratories and Bedaux International demonstrated a new type of camera that would "permit the photographing of the element of time in human labor for the first time in the history of motion pictures without the use of a clock." This new camera would align an exact analysis of every motion in the performance and the time required to perform a specific task. The president of the Bedaux company in New York, Douglas E. Keogh, remarked that it would be a great value to industry. (*New York Times*, September 21, 1934.)

[20] In a June 1943 letter written by the French poet and war hero Antoine de Saint-Exupéry to General Antoine Béthouart, he called life in the twentieth century the era of advertising, the Bedaux System, and totalitarian regimes, writing this: "Man has become a robot on the assembly line of the Bedaux System." Shortly after, Saint-Exupéry was killed while flying on a mission for the Free French Forces.

within the new leadership of the Third Reich. With the National Socialist Party in power in Germany, in 1933 Bedaux's German office had been closed down. But on December 29, 1933, Bedaux wrote to client Willy Tischbein, then director of Continental Gummi-Werke, to say he was prepared to "reorganize a new Bedaux Company strictly in accordance with the directives of the new government and very possibly under the leadership of a man high in authority in German affairs at the present time."[21]

To Bedaux, the Nazi's New World Order was an attractive alternative to capitalism and communism, but this belief eventually led to his downfall. Problems arose for Bedaux's companies in the United States and Britain in 1937-38 as a consequence of what we can call the Bedaux-Windsor affair. As our story progresses, we'll discuss this in detail.

What we can say about Bedaux's talents is that he was imaginative, and in many ways a visionary. He foresaw great potential in trade between European and United States industries and the emerging Middle East oil wealth and the low-priced textile industry in India. He saw them all brought together through the strength of the Bedaux System. Bedaux the entrepreneur was always seeking an edge, along with leverage with his clients and his contacts in the political-industrial world.[22]

The war had started, but it was still the "phony war" period, so Bedaux continued to expand his empire. In

---

[21] Erkner, *Zeitschrift,* 139-158.

[22] Willy Tischbein was a shareholder in the first version of Bedaux International, which had been organized in the United States in 1927. Bedaux often turned to leading business personalities and gave them board positions, along with fees that went with such titles. In today's terminology, this would be called a "kickback."

March 1940, a Bedaux company was launched in neutral Portugal when the president of the council of ministers, António de Oliveira Salazar, requested that a study be made of his country's economy.

French armaments minister Raoul Dautry assigned Bedaux to travel to Spain in the early months of 1940 to obtain Spanish steel for France, but a deal couldn't be made; although iron ore supplies were adequate, coal was in short supply. But on this mission, Bedaux met with French Ambassador Marshal Pétain and General Francisco Franco, the dictator of Spain. Soon thereafter, Bedaux opened an office in Madrid.

HIS TRAVELS

Bedaux was a near-constant traveler, a man in motion, restless, curious, a trailblazer with lavish style—a perfect cover for possible espionage.

In the fall of 1926, Bedaux and his party traveled to British Columbia to hunt and explore. This trip was a forerunner to his so-called Champagne Safari, a much larger expedition he undertook years later.

From late 1929 to early 1930, Bedaux embarked on a five-month, 9500-mile African journey during which he was the first to cross the continent at its widest point in a motorized vehicle. His party started in Kenya, traveling from Mombasa to Nairobi, then went south to Tanganyika (now Tanzania) and the Serengeti Plain. They returned to Nairobi before journeying on to southern Uganda, where they crossed the equator. Next it was 900 miles to the Nile, to Tonga, then to El Obeid 300 miles distant; 260 miles from El Fasher to En Nahud; 700 miles to Melfi in Nigeria; and 400 miles to Fort-Lamy; from Fort-Lamy to Kano, another 500 miles; then 600 miles to Niamey, where the party followed the Niger river to Gao. From here they moved on to Reggan and Rhad and, finally, to journey's end in Casablanca.

Imagine the planning and equipment required for this trek, and Bedaux's willpower to initiate it. What was the mission? What was the reason for this dangerous undertaking? Bedaux was always interested in spreading his name and gaining fame. There was certainly a commercial side to his endeavors—was there perhaps another?[23]

In 1934, Bedaux went on his famous exploration trip to the Canadian Rockies that would later be known as the Champagne Safari. It was a four-hundred-mile journey in five half-track vehicles made by Citroën on a route that no one had ever before taken, not even on horseback or on foot. Their objective was to cross Canada from south to north—that is, to explore the area between Edmonton and Telegraph Creek on the Stikine River, and to continue down the Stikine Valley to Wrangell, Alaska—but they didn't achieve their goal. The Champagne Safari began on July 6, 1934, and ended in late October.

Floyd Crosby, the well-known Hollywood cameraman who later won an Oscar for *High Noon*, was hired to film the big show. It was indeed a big show, complete with dozens of extras and some carefully staged dramatic moments, all for maximum effect. The expedition cost $250,000,[24] and this was in the midst of a worldwide depression.

---

[23]   In a cable to the *New York Times*, Bedraux announced he had completed an automobile run from Mombasa to Casablanca. "Our cars being the first to cross Africa from ocean to ocean north of the equator and through the Sahara Desert...a triumph for American automobile manufacturers." Bedaux had used one Buick and five Fords. (*New York Times*, April 17, 1930.)

[24] $250,000 in 1934 is equivalent to $4.1 million in 2011!

In an article dated May 30, 1934, the *Toronto Star* quoted Bedaux: "Our roadway (halfway to Great Slave) may be continued all the way east in order that radium ore can be brought out by tractor." So there *was* an economic dimension to the expensive journey. Was Bedaux interested in the uranium ore deposits found in Canada? We now know that Canada's uranium ore is high grade, and that the deposits represent 30 percent of the world's total. German scientists had been engaged in nuclear research for many years at the famous Max Planck and Kaiser Wilhelm Institutes. Was Bedaux on a mission, or was he merely an adventurer and publicity hound? Probably a bit of both.

There is now a Mount Bedaux in northern British Columbia, and in 1995 an award-winning documentary titled *The Champagne Safari* was released. All this to recognize Bedaux's failed adventure.[25]

In June 1935, Bedaux visited the world's largest oil refinery, Abadan, in southwestern Iran, while on assignment for the Anglo-Iranian Oil Company. As we shall see, this intimate knowledge of one of Great Britain's key resources would later play an important role in the Nazi regime's war planning.

Following that was one of Bedaux's most interesting trips: a six-week visit to the Soviet Union in early 1936. His visit coincided with the Stakhonovite movement, in which the Communist party celebrated individual workers' record-setting achievements in coal-mining production. Some claim that the Soviet Union's Stakhonovite coal

---

[25] It was a critique of the documentary in the *New York Times* on Nov. 3, 1996, that aroused my interest in Charles Eugene Bedaux.

production increases were inspired by the Bedaux System.[26] The Soviets welcomed the well-known production expert and gave him full VIP treatment, including meetings with important officials and various plant visits. This kind of knowledge would have been of interest to an intelligence service.

There were many trips during the intervening years. This book's purpose, however, isn't to cover all of Bedaux's activities, but to single out the activities that show some connection with enhancing his espionage potential.[27]

In 1939, while in South Africa on a business trip, Bedaux decided to drive from Capetown to Cairo, a 9500-mile trip. He and his wife, Fern, departed on March 14 in a Ford Anglia, and they arrived in Cairo three months later, on June 18. The recently completed road in the Belgian Congo made the journey possible. En route, Bedaux visited mines and factories, which added to his reputation as an expert on Africa.

Germany had been interested in Africa since the days of Kaiser Wilhelm II, who dreamed of establishing colonies there. Bedaux's expertise, therefore, was to be of great interest to various circles in Nazi Germany.

---

[26] Harry Pollitt, the British Communist Party leader, was concerned about how the "speed-up king's" visit would be received by his membership. (Andrew Thorpe, *The British Communist Party*, 229.)

[27] Stalin said, "American efficiency is the indomitable force which neither knows nor recognizes obstacles... the combination of the Russian revolutionary sweep with American efficiency is the essence of Leninism." (Thomas P. Hughes, *American Genesis*.) Did Bedaux meet with Stalin? Will we ever know?

WINNING NEW FRIENDS
AND INFLUENCE

When Hitler came to power in March 1933, Bedaux's company was in jeopardy. The name alone of Hitler's party—the National Socialists—revealed its opinion of free enterprise: industry and commerce were to be conscripted to serve the state. In the party's eyes, Bedaux competed with Dr. Robert Ley's Labor Front Ministry, which was charged with increasing worker productivity. Bedaux was soon banned from doing business in Germany.

But Charles Bedaux wasn't easily stymied, and he began searching for connections that would let him work under the new government. He asked his friend Josef von Ledebur, a young Austrian-Hungarian nobleman who knew where to find links to the new power brokers, to help reverse the ban.[28] A chain of events soon began that put Bedaux in

---

[28]   Josef von Ledebur and his brother, Friedrich, both worked with Bedaux for many years. Friedrich von Ledebur accompanied Bedaux on a number of trips, and in the 1930s he emigrated to the United States, where he became a Hollywood movie actor.

contact with the upper echelon of men leading Germany. Almost without exception (Hjalmar Schacht probably had his doubts), these leaders were intrigued by Bedaux's personality and wealth.

To begin his mission to reverse Bedaux's ban, von Ledebur did the logical thing: he turned to Germany's largest and most influential bank, Deutsche Bank, which had been used by the Bedaux consultancy since 1929. The bank had been founded after the Franco-Prussian War of 1870-71, and had been a key player in the German economy ever since.

With Hitler's rise to power and the consequent removal of non-Aryan management, Emil Georg von Stauss, a former board member and now a member of the supervisory board, became the bank's unofficial representative to the new government.

M. M. Laemmle, a manager in Bedaux's German office, had first asked the bank for assistance in 1933 by writing to von Stauss. Von Stauss in turn suggested that Dr. Rudolf Gleimius, who had been the bank's United States representative in the late 1920s, look into the matter.[29] Gleimius turned to yet another bank official for assistance: Ernst Alfred von Lewinski, a newly minted member of the Nazi Party.

Their efforts up till then were not very successful, but with Josef von Ledebur now on the Bedaux payroll, a new start was made. Through social contacts, von Ledebur

---

[29] Gleimius continued his banking career after the war: in 1947 he was appointed by the victorious Allied governments to collect on the loans made by the three big German banks, and in 1950 he became president of the executive board at Berliner Zentralbank. (Lothar Gall, *The Deutsche Bank*, 393, 396.)

approached von Stauss once again and emphasized Bedaux's usefulness in business and political circles in France, Britain, and the United States, and a meeting between von Stauss and Bedaux finally took place in Berlin in December 1935. Bedaux charmed and impressed von Stauss, and thus the two began their collaboration.

Von Stauss would play an important role in Bedaux's activities in Germany during the 1930s. With the given name Emil Georg Stauss, he was born on October 6, 1877, in the Stuttgart area. His father, a schoolteacher, sent sixteen-year-old Stauss to work as an apprentice at a local Stuttgart bank, where he stayed until 1898. He then took a clerical position at Deutsche Bank in Berlin. He was fortunate: because he could take stenography, he became an assistant to Georg von Siemens, a member of the management board. In 1915, Stauss himself was promoted to the management board, thus continuing his storybook career.

In December 1915, Stauss married Karin Elisabeth von Mueller, daughter of Admiral von Mueller, the Kaiser's chief of the naval staff. Georg Stauss was now at the top of German society. The King of Wurttemburg awarded him the patent of nobility in 1917, making him Ritter von Stauss. After Germany's defeat in the First World War, von Stauss was appointed to the German delegation that negotiated the Treaty of Versailles.

At Deutsche Bank, von Stauss became interested in Romania's oil industry and, more specifically, ways to ensure Germany's access to this vital resource. In 1903, Deutsche Bank acquired shares in Sterua Romano, the Romanian oil company that controlled important oil deposits in the Carpathian Mountains. Von Stauss joined Sterua Romano in 1905 and became its general director in 1914. He was now the bank's oil specialist—and also became the general director of Deutsche Petroleum A.G., which had investments in Persia.[30]

Von Stauss was also interested in these so-called modern industries: automotive, air transport, film, and synthetic fibers. All in all, he served on more than sixty supervisory boards, including those of Daimler Benz, BMW, and Lufthansa.

In 1932, because of a financial mishap at a brewery where von Stauss was chairman and the resulting embarrassment to the bank, von Stauss resigned from the bank's management board, but was elected to the supervisory board.

The banking business during the Third Reich—and even before, late in the Weimar years, when speculation grew that the Nazis would come to power—had a need for the "proper" political connections. Georg von Stauss was destined to play that role for Deutsche Bank.

There was also a political dimension to the banker. In 1930, von Stauss was elected to the Reichstag as a deputy for the liberal-nationalistic *Deutsche Volkspartei* (DVP). Through his positions on corporate boards, he met Hermann Göring, who had been a consultant for BMW in the 1920s, and Eric Milch, who was on the Lufthansa management board. Early in 1931, when von Stauss was a board member of the Reichsbank (Germany's central bank), he introduced former bank president Hjalmar Schacht to Hermann Göring and Adolf Hitler. It was also at von Stauss's home in Berlin on December 5, 1931, that Hitler met Frederic

---

[30] Deutsche Petroleum A.G. was sold in 1926-31 to Anglo-Persian Oil Company, which would later become Bedaux's client.

Sackett, the American ambassador to Germany. In effect, von Stauss was now a political entrepreneur.[31]

When the Nazis came to power in March 1933, Göring, the president of the Reichstag, appointed von Stauss to the Prussian Staatsrat (state council), and in 1934 to vice president of the Reichstag.[32]

In addition, von Stauss held positions in key cultural and academic associations. He was honorary president of the German-French Society, whose members came from the business, academic, and media world, and for which there was a French counterpart. This brought him in contact with Otto Abetz and Julius Westrick.[33]

Von Stauss was also vice president of the *Deutsche Akademie*, which was founded in 1925 with an educational mission. In 1933, however, the mission changed to promoting German language and culture abroad as part of a propaganda effort.

Georg von Stauss met Charles Bedaux in December 1935. Bedaux, the super salesman, enchanted von Stauss, like he did so many others. Von Stauss and Bedaux had a great deal in common: both had achieved fame and fortune without much formal education. Marrying well was also quite helpful for them. Von Stauss recognized the potential Bedaux represented for the Third Reich. He

---

[31] "Politics with the new regime had been delegated to von Stauss. He managed the team's most sensitive customers, film, theater, automobiles, synthetic fibers." (Ibid., 308.)

[32] Vice president of the Reichstag was a nominal position.

[33] Abetz and Westrick were assigned to France as members of the *Büro* Ribbentrop, a party organization with a mission to win friends and influence for the Third Reich in France. Both men would later play interesting roles in Charles Bedaux's activities during the occupation of France.

became Bedaux's mentor in navigating the complex world of Hitler's Germany. Von Stauss is described as being directed to "doing business and making money, and not on a desire for explicit political power."[34] Bedaux looked at Hitler's New World Order as a means to an end, a new path for commercial success, if only one could find the proper channels.

On April 29, 1937, von Stauss—along with Otto Abetz and Julius Westrick—visited Chateau de Candé, Bedaux's magnificent estate near Tours, France. Von Stauss, who owned Burg Schlitz, a sixty-room castle on 4600 acres of land in Mecklenburg, was impressed.[35] Bedaux spoke of his inventions in the automotive and film industries, and later sent these inventions to von Stauss to evaluate, but neither he nor Daimler Benz nor UFA found the inventions to be practical.[36]

Both Bedaux and von Stauss agreed that the way to overcome government objections was to launch a new company in Berlin, to be named *Gesellschaft für Wirtschaftsberatung* (GFW), which would employ the Bedaux System. Heinrich Schlindwein would run the new company—he was a German engineer who had worked in Bedaux's German office until it was shut down, and then serviced clients from the Holland office. Rather than being a company shareholder, Bedaux International (of which Bedaux owned 100 percent) would receive 15 percent of

---

[34] Ibid., 318.

[35] Burg Schlitz, built in 1825 and acquired by von Stauss in 1932, is now a hotel.

[36] UFA was Germany's motion picture company, of which von Stauss was a shareholder. He was also on the supervisory boards of UFA and Daimler-Benz. (Deutsche Bank Archive)

the revenue. Von Stauss would be on the board and receive five hundred RM per month, until a hundred thousand RM was paid. He was also to serve as the *Schiedsrichter*, or referee, when contractual disputes arose.

The Deutsche Bank archive brought to my attention an archived file of correspondence relating to von Stauss and Bedaux, and what it says about the close relationship between the two men is most revealing. Von Stauss presented Bedaux's proposal to manufacture explosives by using a byproduct of hemp production to the top echelon of the government and military. For six months, from May to October 1937, von Stauss was in contact with, among others, General Karl Becker, head of the research council for the armed forces, which was responsible overseeing research for the high command.[37]

A lab tested a sample of the hemp byproduct that Bedaux had passed on to von Stauss. A filmstrip was made that showed production at Amhempco Company in Danville, Illinois. Zellstoff Waldhof, a major cellulose manufacturer in Germany, was asked to evaluate Bedaux's estimate of German hemp production, and in its findings it proclaimed that the writer could not really be serious, "*Kann nicht ernsthaft gemeint sein.*" The Waldhof people went to Danville to check out the plant, but were advised not to invest in it.

This illustrates how Bedaux, the super salesman and perhaps an investor in the Danville operation, was already close to von Stauss. Bedaux's motive was clear: he wanted to gain favor with von Stauss's circle. This mystery, however, remains: Why would von Stauss continue to be in

---

[37]   Professor Karl Heinrich Emil Becker, 1879-1940, committed suicide allegedly after being criticized by Hitler.

contact with Bedaux when he knew of Bedaux's tendency to exaggerate his expertise? Was old-fashioned greed the answer? (The possibility that there was indeed a Trans-Africa Company in which these two and others were involved now seems more likely; the Trans-Africa Company will be covered in a later chapter.)

Another interesting aspect of the von Stauss-Bedaux relationship involved the American branch of the von Stauss family. Georg von Stauss had a brother who had emigrated to the United States before the First World War.[38] That brother's son, George Stauss, a recent university graduate, went to Germany in 1934 to visit von Stauss, and didn't return home until September 1939, at the start of the Second World War.[39]

In January 1936, George Stauss met Charles and Fern Bedaux at a dinner party at von Stauss' Berlin-Dahlem home.[40] In May 1936, Georg von Stauss introduced young George Stauss to Heinrich Schlindwein, Bedaux's German partner, who hired him to work in Bedaux's Dutch office. After five days of training, George Stauss joined a team at a textile finishing plant, and he continued on-and-off work for Bedaux during his stay in Europe, including assignments in Austria and Hungary.[41]

Young George Stauss also studied at the *Hochschule für Welthandel* in Vienna, earning his doctorate in August

---

[38]   Von Stauss had two other brothers: Adolf, director of the Ruttgers Werk, and Eugen, finance director of UFA.

[39]   The information relating to his activities came from an Internet manuscript called "Part II: Five years in Europe 1934-1939."

[40]   This was probably a mistake in date. Bedaux was visiting the USSR at the time.

[41]   Bedaux employed a number of White Russians in Holland.

1939 after completing his dissertation titled "*Das Bedaux System und Seine Wirtschaftlichkeit.*" He then returned to the States.

The banker Georg von Stauss introduced Bedaux to Annie Höfken-Hempel, an attractive young sculptress who just happened to be the mistress of Dr. Hjalmar Schacht. Dr. Schacht once again headed the Reichsbank, Germany's central bank. Höfken-Hempel advised Bedaux to rent a home in the Berchtesgaden area, which was in the neighborhood of Hitler and other leading players in the Party and government.[42]

Von Stauss did whatever he could to help Charles Bedaux receive government approval for GFW, his new company. But the government's bone of contention was the 15 percent commission that was to be charged for the use of the Bedaux System. The need quickly became apparent for some high-powered legal advice—there had, of course, been other lawyers involved in the preparation of contracts and such—but no progress. His new company was functioning, but Bedaux's 15 percent commission was not approved.

Early in 1937, Annie Höfken-Hempel arranged for Bedaux to have dinner with Hjalmar Schacht, and they discussed how to get approval for the GFW contract.[43] At the time, Schacht was on leave from his position as the minister of economics. He resigned from this position

---

[42] Bedaux and the French ambassador to Germany, André François-Poncet, later co-sponsored an exhibition of Annie Höfken-Hempel's work in Paris. The exhibition included busts of Charles and Fern Bedaux.

[43] Schacht was never a member of the Nazi Party. After the attempt on Hitler's life, he was imprisoned by the regime in the last months of the war, was tried with the group of leading Nazis in Nuremburg, and was acquitted.

in December 1937, but continued to be president of the Reichsbank. Schacht suggested that a fifty thousand dollar donation might help—twenty thousand to the Nazi Party and thirty thousand to the Party's winter relief fund—and Bedaux was quick to oblige. But this, too, was not enough to grease the wheels and get the contract approved.

Once again, von Stauss intervened and arranged a meeting between Bedaux and Joachim von Ribbentrop, the Reich's foreign minister. On August 21, 1939, along with von Stauss and Otto Abetz, von Ribbentrop's special advisor on France, Bedaux visited the foreign minister at his Obersalzberg home. Also on that fateful day, von Ribbentrop received Hitler's order to go to Moscow to sign the non-aggression pact with the Soviets, freeing the way for the invasion of Poland. [44]

---

[44] Von Stauss died on December 11, 1942. His role on the supervisory board had been a "kind of political insurance" for Deutsche Bank, and on his death, relations with the state and party became much more difficult. (Lothar Gall, *The Deutsche Bank*, 318.)

THE LAWYER

Before leaving for Moscow, von Ribbentrop advised Bedaux to appoint Gerhard Alois Westrick, a German lawyer specializing in international law, as his lawyer. Bedaux quickly followed his advice. He returned to Berlin and met with Westrick for the first time on August 23, 1939.

Westrick, born in 1889, was severely wounded in the First World War and lost part of a leg. In 1921 he joined Heinrich Friedrich Albert's law firm, specializing in international corporate law.[45] Among their clients were

---

[45] Albert (1874-1960) had been in the United States from 1914 to 1917 under the cover of a commercial attaché. He collected money from pro-German sources to support the espionage-sabotage activities under the control of the German military attaché Franz von Papen. On July 24, 1915, Albert left a briefcase with incriminating documents in a New York City subway car. Although embarrassing for Albert, he stayed in the States until 1917. In 1923, German Chancellor Gustav Stresemann asked Albert to help form a government, but was unsuccessful. Albert left the law firm in 1936 to become chairman of Ford Germany. After the fall of France, he also assumed the chairmanship of Ford France.

Kodak, Ford, Texas Oil, General Motors, General Milk, and ITT. Westrick became the chairman of ITT in Germany, and played a key role in the company's acquisitions throughout Eastern Europe.

Bedaux and his company, GFW, had been using the Graf von der Goltz-Rudolph Patsch law firm, but it hadn't been able to get the Ministries of Foreign Affairs and Economics to allow Bedaux to do business in Germany.[46]

When Bedaux hired Westrick as his lawyer, things began to happen immediately. By November 1, the Ministry of Foreign Affairs approved the contract that allowed Bedaux to work in Germany. Walther Funk, the minister of economic affairs, had been the stumbling block. Funk was weak, and wasn't about to give a different opinion than that of the powerful labor minister, Robert Ley. Their main objection was that the 15 percent fee for the use of the Bedaux System would leave the country—with the stringent currency controls in place, this was a non-starter. The parties found a compromise, agreeing to reduce the fee to 7.5 percent during the war years and to keep that money in Germany. The Ministry of Economic Affairs approved Bedaux's GFW contract in February 1940.

Westrick had been called up for service in the officer reserve in 1936, but was rejected due to his war injuries. He wanted to serve his country, however, and expressed an interest in intelligence work. He had strong contacts in the

---

[46] The information that follows on the Bedaux-Westrick contacts is based on BAKoblenz, Bestand 1200, Band 1045, *Nachlass Gerhard Alois Westrick*. The German words "Bestand" and "Band" mean "File" and "Volume," respectively, and "Nachlass" describes the collection of manuscripts, notes, correspondence, and so on left behind when a scholar dies.

international business world, and wanted to exploit those connections. Upon meeting Bedaux, Westrick recognized the intelligence potential of his new French-American client, and quickly recommended Bedaux to the top echelon of German intelligence. (In intelligence terms, Westrick was a "spotter.")

Westrick first approached Colonel Brinkmann of the Abwehr, Germany's intelligence arm of Germany's general staff. This was followed by a meeting with Brinkmann's boss, *Kapitän zur See* Leopold Bürkner, who was responsible for foreign intelligence as chief of Department I. Westrick also had several exchanges about Bedaux's intelligence value with Dr. Halvor Sudeck at a Berlin address: Berlin-Halensee, Paulsborner Str. 83 B.[47]

The last correspondence from Westrick to Sudeck was dated March 2, 1942. It contained information from Bedaux about Marshal Pétain and his group and their activities with

---

[47] Dr. Halvor Sudeck (1902-1958) received his PhD in 1930 from *Technische Hochschule* in Braunschweig for his dissertation, "Die Erschliessung von Industriegelände," or "Development of Land for Industry." I haven't been able to identify where Dr. Sudeck fit in the intelligence picture. Sudeck may have been a member of the War Economy and Armaments Department, whose chief was General Georg Thomas. The various sections of this department were headed by military men but staffed by highly qualified civilian specialists.

the French Legion in North Africa—in particular, details on key personnel in the French colonial administration.[48]

In Westrick's notes to Sudeck and Bürkner, he stated how important his position as chairman of the German ITT board was for collecting intelligence. He referred to his ability to influence decisions on what could be shipped from ITT plants in Hungary to Turkey. Turkey had a treaty with the UK and a non-aggression treaty with Germany, and remained neutral for most of the war. It was the principal supplier of chromium to Germany. Without this critical metal, Germany's war material production would have come to a screeching halt.[49]

An interesting question to be resolved is this: What was Bedaux's Constantinople office up to during this period? Franz von Papen was an old hand at intrigue, and he was the German ambassador to Turkey. Indeed, Bedaux and von Papen had met in the early 1930s.[50] In 1930 Turkey had a population of almost 18 million, of which 70 percent worked in agriculture. Turkish President Mustafa Kemal Atatürk had been dedicated to making Turkey a modern, industrial state—and the Bedaux company had a role to play.

In a letter to Sudeck, Westrick stated that he had specifically received permission from Admiral Canaris's staff

---

48   Bürkner was promoted to admiral in 1943, and assumed command of what remained of the Abwehr after the arrest of Admiral Canaris in 1944. Wilhelm Canaris (Jan. 1, 1887-April 9, 1945) headed the Abwehr from 1935-1944, and was executed at the Flossenbürg concentration camp shortly before the end of the war.

49   See Albert Speer, *Inside the Third Reich: Memoirs*.

50   Jonathan Steinberg, *The Deutsche Bank*.

to keep meeting Bedaux, whom he believed was an honest friend of Germany.[51]

Westrick's brother Julius was on the staff of German Ambassador Otto Abetz after the occupation of France, and another brother, Ludger, headed the German aluminum industry under Herman Göring.[52]

In January 1940 the German government awarded Westrick the title of *Wehrwirtschaftsführer* in recognition of his contribution to Germany's war effort.[53] This honor was followed by an assignment from Foreign Minister von Ribbentrop to travel to the United States in March 1940 (under cover of commercial counselor to the German embassy) to learn about important American business leaders and to influence their view toward Germany and the war. He was also asked to explore the possibility of getting a $5 billion loan for the Third Reich once peace was established. Along with his young family, Westrick traveled via Siberia and still-neutral Japan to avoid interception by the British Navy. They arrived in the United States on March 7 and stayed until August 23.

In many ways, Westrick's assignment duplicated that of his former senior partner, Heinrich Albert, who had been in the United States on an intelligence mission during the First World War. Before departing, Westrick proposed to General Georg Thomas, *Wehrwirtschaft-und Vermessungsamt*, that he could use his influence on shipments of communications

---

[51] Most of Westrick's activities are based on the Westrick file in the BAKoblenz.

[52] Ludger Westrick (1894-1990) also served on West German Chancellor Ludwig Erhard's cabinet from 1963 to 1966.

[53] Four hundred people received this award between 1939 and 1944.

equipment from ITT Hungary to Turkey to guaranty delivery of vital chrome ore from that neutral country.

For his mission he was given a salary of $3,300 per month, and had $4,000 petty cash on deposit, which was not nearly enough to cover travel and entertainment expenses. But he had additional support from Texas Oil Company, whose CEO, Torkild "Cap" Rieber, had for some time been violating the Neutrality Act by selling oil to the Nazis in support of their naval activities.[10] Rieber provided Westrick with offices in New York and paid his expenses for a house in Westchester County, along with a Buick automobile.

Westrick met with his American clients and found them supportive of the Third Reich's political goals; they were probably motivated by their desire to protect their investments in Germany and the European continent, and to block the spread of Bolshevism. They wanted to see President Roosevelt defeated in the upcoming election. Old Henry Ford (a Hitler favorite) even advised Westrick that the Nazis should attack Republican candidate Wendel Wilkie, Roosevelt's opponent, to get more votes. With a Wilkie victory, claimed Ford, America's foreign policy would be more favorable to Germany.

But Charles Bedaux was never very far from Westrick's mind. In a May 13, 1940, letter to his Berlin office, Westrick stressed how important Bedaux was to the German cause. Important American businessmen had confirmed this opinion.

The highlight of Westrick's effort to sway decision-makers was a celebration dinner sponsored by Cap Rieber at the Waldorf Astoria on June 26, 1940, the day after France surrendered to the Nazis. Among those present were Col. Sosthenes Behn, CEO of ITT; Ralph Beaver Strassburger, a financier and publisher from Pennsylvania;

James D. Mooney, head of General Motor's international operations and recipient of the Golden Eagle award from Adolf Hitler; Edsel Ford of the Ford automobile family; and P. D. Wagoner, president of Underwood.

At about the same time that Westrick arrived in the United States, the British appointed a new chief of the Secret Intelligence Service, or MI6, for North America: "Quiet Canadian" William Stephenson. To MI6, Westrick's mission could reduce projected U.S. aid to Britain, and had to be stopped. Stephenson was soon on the trail of the Westrick-Rieber team, and he blew their cover through a series of well-placed leaks in the American press. A *Time* magazine article from July 8, 1940, titled "German Tempter," described Westrick as "simply a scout and atmosphere conjurer, sent over to feel out Big Business Sentiment and plant some seeds." Public opinion pressure and official embarrassment then led to Westrick being declared a persona non-grata, and his subsequent departure from the United States on August 23, 1940. He returned to Germany via the Pacific Ocean, and continued to service United States clients and maintain contact with Bedaux.

While Westrick was in the United States, the Ministry of Economic Affairs approved Bedaux's GFW contract in which he would receive (and keep in Germany) 7.5 percent of revenue during the war's duration.

In his report to the foreign ministry upon his return to Germany, Westrick said that the views of the Americans he met would be considered treason in other countries, but in the United States, it was "just doing business."

As our story progresses, Westrick will appear again. Was Westrick the first to recognize Bedaux's intelligence value to the Reich? Doubtful.

ROYAL FRIENDS

While Bedaux was going through all kinds of machinations to operate once again in Germany, he was about to become involved in a crisis that would shake Great Britain's royal family.

Edward David, the glamorous and popular Prince of Wales, became King Edward VIII on January 10, 1936, upon the death of his father, George V. He was known as a swinging bachelor, but he became enamored by Mrs. Wallis Simpson, an American divorcée who was then married to Ernest Aldrich Simpson.[54] She was a woman with a past that, rumor had it, was not too savory. Edward was determined to marry the lady come what may, but ran into unrelenting opposition from Prime Minister Baldwin and the Archbishop of Canterbury. He was advised to enter into a morganatic marriage with Mrs. Simpson, but Edward was determined to make her his queen.

To avoid a constitutional crisis, he abdicated—gave up the throne—on December 10, 1936. Until then, the British

---

[54] Simpson (1895-1958) was a Harvard-educated shipping executive.

press had been silent about the unfolding royal drama. But the German government, of course, was very much aware of what was happening. Leopold von Hoesch, the German ambassador in London, had been reporting diligently on the unfolding events.[55] Joachim von Ribbentrop, the future foreign minister, replaced von Hoesch as ambassador, and he was quick to recognize the need to win Mrs. Simpson's heart and mind. Ever the gallant, von Ribbentrop reportedly sent her a bouquet of seventeen roses every day.[56]

During King Edward's short reign, the re-arming of Germany became evident. The Wehrmacht's march into the Rhineland on March 7, 1936, which the British-French alliance viewed as a barrier to German aggression, led to a call for greater expenditures for the armed forces.[57] The king, who had shown signs of a strong pro-German bias, considered this fear to be greatly exaggerated. He was of German ancestry and spoke the language fluently—some would say better than English. He considered the new regime in Germany a strong barrier to Soviet communist expansion to the west.

When Mussolini invaded Ethiopia in October 1935, Edward believed that the invasion helped bring that

---

[55] Leopold von Hoesch died in April 1936, and some believed the Nazis murdered him for his anti-regime views.

[56] Ambassador Leopold von Hoesch (1881-1936) had commented on Edward's pro-German views in reports to the German foreign minister. In 1934, when Edward was the Prince of Wales, von Hoesch had repeated that he was favorably disposed to the "New Germany."

[57] Under the 1919 Treaty of Versailles, Germany was forbidden to have fortifications in the area. The Locarno Treaty of 1925 signed by Germany, France, Italy, and Britain confirmed this status.

backward nation into a modern world, and he liked the discipline that these two fascist states represented. He felt that this discipline was lacking in Britain and in the other democracies of Europe. One of Edward's great admirers and supporters was Sir Oswald Mosley, leader of the British fascist movement.[58]

With the nickname "Nazi Duke," Karl Edward, the Duke of Sachsen-Coburg Gotha and a ranking member of the SA, was another link to the fascist world and an Edward favorite. They met in London in 1936, and Foreign Secretary Anthony Eden is quoted as saying about Edward the former king: "He knew little and interfered much."[59] John Aird, aid (equerry) to the king, said that Edward "prided himself on being born a salesman."[60] We know what happens when two salesmen meet: why, they sell one another. This, too, may have been a factor when the ex-king—bitter because of his family's and the British government's refusal to give his wife the title of Her Royal Highness—sat down with Charles Bedaux to discuss the future.

The relationship between Edward and Mrs. Simpson was described as that of "mother and child," or "mistress-slave,"[61] and it was said that Edward's every decision "was subordinate to her will." What she wanted was to be married to a king,

---

[58] Mosley and his wife were incarcerated for a time during the Second World War, charged with being a security threat. They had married in Berlin in 1936 at Goebbels' home, with Hitler as an honored guest. After the war, the Mosleys spent half their time in France, where they often were the Windsors' dinner guests.

[59] J. Bryan III and Charles J. V. Murphy, *The Windsor Story*, 206.

[60] Ibid., 207.

[61] Ibid., 250.

and when this could not be, what then? Did she push the duke into almost committing treason to bring him back to the throne with the help of Hitler? Was Bedaux destined to be the courier to bring this about?

Alex Hardinge, who was close to Edward, best expresses the danger of Edward's relationship with Mrs. Simpson: "As time went on, it became clear that every decision, big or small, was subordinated to her will . . . . It was she who filled his thoughts at all times, she alone who mattered, before her the affairs of state sank into insignificance."[62]

After his abdication, Edward left for Schloss Enzesfeld in Austria, where German intelligence monitored his phone calls, discerned his mood, and detected his resentment.[63]

The question of where the wedding of Edward and Mrs. Simpson would take place needed to be addressed. Mrs. Simpson was staying with the Rogers family on the French Riviera, but that was thought to be a playground and not acceptable for the former king of Great Britain's wedding. They eventually chose Bedaux's castle, Chateau de Candé, for the wedding, and there are different ideas about how this decision was made. One is that Bedaux directly approached Herman Rogers, Wallis Simpson's friend and host, whom Bedaux had entertained at the chateau a couple of years before. (Rogers' brother, Edmund, was Bedaux's financial advisor in New York.) Another speculation is that Fern Bedaux wrote to Wallis Simpson as one American woman to another, and offered a refuge from the journalists who were searching for news around her Riviera retreat.

---

[62] Hardinge (1894-1960) had been assistant private secretary of George V and was appointed Edward's private secretary.

[63] Ibid., 351.

Wallis Warfield Simpson moved to Chateau de Candé in early March of 1937.

Knowing what we know about the Abwehr's monitoring of Edward's telephone in Schloss Enzesfeld, we could also construct a case for scheme by German intelligence to gain control of the situation by using Bedaux as an instrument. Was Bedaux already a de facto German agent? If the Abwehr were involved, they would have known that Herman Rogers would ask his brother Edmund to check on Bedaux's bona fides, and an all-clear would've been forthcoming. So was it innocent coincidence, or was it an intelligence plot? In any case, someone dropped the ball. Bedaux was about to host the bride of the former king of the British Empire; why were there no warning signals about his personality and character?

Chateau de Candé was built in 1508, and was located eight miles (thirteen kilometers) from Tours. Bedaux bought it in 1927 for $32,000, and spent $1 million to restore and modernize it. It now had swimming pools, a nine-hole golf course, tennis courts, and an organ worth $40,000 (and which to this day is considered a masterpiece of its kind).

Edward joined Wallis Simpson at the chateau on May 4, after her divorce became final. Both consoled one another about how they had been treated by their respective countries. She told him, "I have ceased to be an American. I'll make my life with you outside the boundaries of nationality."[64] The marriage took place on June 3, 1937, and the friendship between Bedaux and the Duke of Windsor was launched soon afterward. If Bedaux was not yet in league with German intelligence, he was certainly quick to recognize how to gain social ground to the benefit of his

---

[64] Ibid., 360.

business enterprise. The Bedauxs presented the newlyweds with the statute titled "Love" by German artist Annie Höfkin-Hempel, who was Hjalmar Schacht's mistress.[65]

The final blow to the duke's pride came on his wedding day, when he was told that his wife-to-be wouldn't be given the title Her Royal Highness. This blow must have led to many of his questionable future actions.

Bedaux and the duke had a number of private conversations at Candé. From them, this plan evolved to shine the lime light on the Duke of Windsor and to gain recognition for his wife: Why not first visit Nazi Germany, and then visit the United States? Bedaux would organize these visits to study labor in the German dictatorship and the United States, the world's largest democracy. Bedaux would finance the United States visit, an idea that the tight-fisted duke accepted without hesitation. Minister of Labor Robert Ley would sponsor the visit to Germany.

As strange as it seems, a self-made, multi-millionaire French-American had control of a forty-one-year-old former king of the British Empire. And as time went by, the duke was played like a puppet.

Bedaux and Captain Wiedemann, Hitler's military aide, discussed the duke's travel arrangements, and the

---

[65] After the war, West German Chancellor Adenauer commissioned Annie Höfken-Hempel (1900-1965) to create busts of General Eisenhower and Pope John XXXII.

Bedauxs coordinated the trip.[66] The German foreign ministry assigned an English-speaking special attaché to be in attendance, and he was ordered to meet with Fern Bedaux at the Ritz Hotel in Paris on "20 September 1500 hours to receive further instructions."[67]

On October 11, 1937, the Windsors arrived in Berlin, and thus became useful propaganda weapons for the Nazis. Embarrassing moments took place, such as when the duke instinctively threw out his arm in the Nazi salute. He was clearly impressed with the progress that labor had made—the regime's rearmament program ensured full employment.[68]

---

[66] There was an interesting by-play in the Bedaux-Wiedemann exchange. Wiedemann and Hitler had served together in the 16th Bavarian Infantry Regiment in the First World War. Hitler's immediate commanding officer had been a certain Rosenbusch, who happened to be Jewish. Hitler, strangely enough, felt a certain loyalty to the Jewish officer—who in 1918 had recommended Hitler for the Iron Cross First Class—and wanted to help him get out of Germany. Bedaux agreed to hire Rosenbusch, who was an engineer, for his Dutch company. Rosenbusch later moved on to Bedaux's Turkish company. During the Second World War he returned to Holland, fought with the Underground, was captured, and was believed to have died in a Nazi camp.

[67] State Secretary Hans George von Mackensen on September 17, 1937, #553 *German Foreign Policy 1918-1945, Series C 1933-37*, page 1132.

[68] Throughout the trip, the duchess was greeted as "Her Royal Highness" rather than "Her Grace," which British crown would have preferred. Typical headlines in the U.S. press were "German Society to Fete Windsor," (*New York Times,* October 19, 1937.) and "Stuttgart Greets the Windsors Boisterously." (*New York Times,* October 21, 1937.)

Windsor met with all the Nazi leadership, including Hitler, Göring, Himmler, and Goebbels. The meeting with Hitler was private, with only the Führer's interpreter in attendance.[69] The meetings embarrassed the British Crown and government, but this didn't seem to enter into Edward's thought processes.

On November 5, 1937, two weeks after the Windsor visit, Hitler secretly met with General Werner von Fritsch, Erich Räder and Hermann Göring of the armed forces, along with Minister of War Werner von Blomberg and Foreign Minister Konstantin von Neurath. Hitler outlined his strategy for the future, in which restrictions on espionage against Britain were lifted,[70] and Colonel Friedrich Hossbach, Hitler's military adjutant, wrote a memorandum listing the salient points of the speech. Hitler's speech showed no desire to align with Britain.[71] He didn't speak of colonial aims and European objectives as political alternatives. He didn't see the British Empire as invincible. Rather, he said Britain would compromise and retreat when faced with a well-armed and determined Reich, and allow Hitler to achieve his real aim: to control Europe by 1943 to 1945.

---

[69] Twenty years after the end of the World War Two, Windsor was quoted as having said, "I never thought that Hitler is such a bad chap."

[70] Paul Leverkühn, *German Military Intelligence*, 93.

[71] Hitler's attitude toward the British was somewhat different in 1934, when in conversation with F. W. Winterbotham, an RAF officer and intelligence member, said "There should be only three major powers in the world, the British Empire as it was, the Americans, and the German Empire of the future. (Winterbotham, *The Nazi Connection*, 53.)

The plan was for the Reich to not confront Britain over overseas territory. Hitler wanted Britain to remain neutral concerning his plans to expand through the continent, and believed this was achievable: perhaps he was encouraged by his discussions with Windsor, especially given the duke's pro-Nazi views.

There was more than one line of thought among the Reich's wider circle engaged in foreign policy. The traditionalists, made up of professional diplomats such as Ernst von Weizsäcker, favored negotiation. Then there was Hjalmar Schacht's team, which favored expansion through "liberal imperialism," by using purchasing power rather military might to expand into southeastern Europe and acquire colonies. Hitler's objectives, however, were Vienna, Prague, and Danzig.

Hitler's interest in gaining colonies for the Reich was merely a bargaining tool to divert attention from his real goal: gaining control of the continent. His real foreign policy aim in the late 1930s was to achieve British neutrality as he moved east and west—and achieve it he did. Sure, he wanted a colonial empire, but only after he conquered Europe and had a worldwide naval presence by the second half of the 1940s. He would then be ready to confront the United States.

In 1938, Fritz Wiedemann, Hitler's personal adjutant, went to London on a secret mission to sound out Lord Halifax and Viscount Rothermere, who were leading political and media figures.[72] The Nazis believed that both men were open to the Reich's desire for closer German-British relations.

By this time, British intelligence considered Bedaux a security risk, and asked the duke to cease all contact with him. But His Royal Highness blithely chose to ignore this request. The relationship between the duke and Bedaux continued—in fact, there is a claim that Bedaux delivered critical military information to Berlin in November 1939 that originated with Windsor.[73]

To understand how the king of the British Empire could show a pro-German bias in 1939, it's helpful to look at Britain's atmosphere. In 1935, Britain had signed a naval agreement with Germany allowing its former enemy to rebuild its fleet.[74] British labor still suffered from the

---

[72] Lord Halifax, a leading figure in the Conservative Party, was foreign affairs minister. Lord Rothermere owned the *London Daily Mail* and *Daily Mirror*. Fritz Wiedemann and Lord Rothermere shared more than an admiration for Hitler—they had the same mistress, Princess Stephanie von Hohenlohe Waldenburg, who by using her feminine wiles acted as an agent for Hitler on more than one occasion. Wiedemann was appointed German consul general in San Francisco in 1939, was declared person non grata in June 1941, and was assigned consul general in Tsiensten, China, for the duration of the war.

[73] Martin Allen, *Hidden Agenda*, 146-8.

[74] The agreement limited German naval tonnage to 35 percent of that of the British Navy. The British didn't consult with France or Italy on the matter, and to Germany, this represented the beginning of an alliance against the French and the USSR. The Germans renounced the agreement in 1939.

economic depression, and feared that communism could gain a strong foothold in their ranks.

The Third Reich under Adolf Hitler represented the New Order and the future to some key members of German industry, who supported the Führer under the belief that he was the solution to their problems. In Britain, there was that country's own fascist organization led by King Edward's friend, Sir Oswald Mosley, whose wife was Winston Churchill's cousin. The British media, including the press moguls Lord Rothermere and Lord Beaverbrook, believed that a strong Germany could act as a defense against the spread of communism from the USSR. Geoffrey Dawson, editor of Britain's leading newspaper, the *London Times*, was another German advocate. German sources kept telling British intelligence that the British Empire had nothing to fear from them, that Germany had no interest in recovering lost colonies, that expansion would be to the east in search of *Lebensraum*, or living space.

There were leaders of the business world who also believed Germany could be a friend if left to its own devices. Among them was Sir Montagu Norman of the Bank of England and Sir Henri Deterding of Shell Oil.[75] Such noteworthies as David Lloyd George, prime minister during the First World War, put it this way: "Hitler, greatest living German, who saved his country from bankruptcy."[76]

---

[75]   Montagu Norman (1871-1950), a close friend of Hjalmar Schacht, came under suspicion for pro-Nazi leanings. He was governor of the Bank of England from 1920-1944. Sir Henri Deterding (1866-1939) donated millions in fuel to the Third Reich.

[76]   Lloyd George met with Hitler on September 4, 1936. *London Daily Express*, November 17, 1936.

The Bedaux offices in New York were in the Chrysler Building, where the Scribner Publishing Company was also located. When Bedaux submitted a manuscript for a medieval novel to Scribner, it landed on the desk of the editor and noted poet John Hall Wheelock. The manuscript was rejected, but a number of meetings followed between the two men in 1936 1937. In talking to the editor, Bedaux candidly admired Hitler as a man of genius, and wanted to write a book demonstrating how Hitler was human. Wheelock quoted Bedaux as having said the whole world is "going to go fascist," and that his friend, the Duke of Windsor, would be "recalled to the throne as dictator."[77]

In the meantime, Bedaux traveled to the United States to prepare the ground for the Windsor visit, which was to begin on November 11—Armistice Day, marking the end of the World War—and conclude in mid-December. He paid a leading New York advertising agency, Arthur Kudner, Inc., to assist in the preparations and public relations. This turned out to be a disaster, however. Labor unions and the press opposed Bedaux and the Windsor visit with great vehemence, and the trip was cancelled.[78] The consequences for Bedaux were severe. His American management team demanded that he eliminate his name from the U.S.

---

[77] Wheelock retired as editor in chief in 1957. (John Hall Wheelock, *The Last Romantic.*)

[78] The Nov. 15, 1937, issue of *Time* magazine described how the visit started with the "arrival in the U.S....of a mephistophelian little Franco-American efficiency expert named Charles E. Bedaux."

operation and, in effect, become a silent partner with 55 percent of the shares.[79]

Bedaux, who had arrived in the United States on November 5, departed on November 10, and would never again return to the U.S. under his own free will.

One would have thought that Windsor, having endured this international embarrassment, would have severed all ties to Bedaux. Unfortunately for the royal reputation, this was not the case. In fact, upon his return to France, the Windsors invited Bedaux to visit them at the Hotel Meurice, their temporary Paris domicile. It was only the beginning of the two men's relationship, which continued until at least November 1939. Fern Bedaux and the Duchess of Windsor allegedly corresponded into 1942.[80]

Although Edward put on the bold front of a happy man, as time went by he became more and more embittered by the treatment he was getting from his family in Britain. Their refusal to bestow his wife with the recognition of Her Royal Highness was key to his disenchantment. He became disenfranchised and vulnerable.

Upon his return from the United States, Bedaux suffered a nervous breakdown. And where did he turn for medical assistance? To Germany—specifically, to a sanatorium located in Bad Reichenhall, where he reportedly became addicted to a potent sleeping medication. Bedaux remained

---

[79] Albert Ramond, the French engineer who was one of the first to be hired by Bedaux, controlled the U.S. operations at this point. It continued to function after the war under the name Albert Ramond and Associates. Ramond made peace with the labor unions, whereas they had despised Bedaux, calling him the "speed-up king." (*Time* magazine, January 19, 1942.)

[80] Jim Christy, *The Price of Power*, 150.

here for almost six months. This would have been an ideal period to be well vetted by German intelligence; perhaps this explains Bedaux's decision to recuperate in Germany.

During his stay at Chateau de Candé, Windsor had received a letter from Oscar Solbert, a retired American army officer who had escorted Edward on his visit to the United States in 1924.[81] Swedish by birth, Solbert proposed a meeting with the wealthy Swedish industrialist Axel Wenner-Gren, who was interested in organizing a world peace movement in which Windsor could play a leading role. Windsor began corresponding with Wenner-Gren, but there was a small catch in this exchange: Wenner-Gren was rumored to be friends with Hermann Göring—whose wife was Swedish and therefore he wasn't your everyday Swedish industrialist.[82]

So we now have an unhappy man in the Duke of Windsor: fascist-friendly (his old friend being Sir Oswald Mosley, leader of the British fascist movement), and open to the lures and traps that Charles Bedaux and Axel Wenner-Gren set for him. There is nothing more dangerous than a not-too-clever man who once had the aura of recognition as the king of the world's greatest empire. Bitter about how his wife was treated—a woman with a "past"—and now searching for any kind of activity, he was a prime target for

---

[81] Oscar Solbert returned to active duty during World War II and served in the European theater as chief of special services.

[82] Axel Wenner-Gren (1881-1961), one of the wealthiest men of the era, made his fortune on the vacuum cleaner, which he made into a household product. He was later on the British and American watch list for trading with the enemy. During the Duke of Windsor's assignment as governor of the Bahamas, he continued to associate with Wenner-Gren.

German intelligence. Here was a man who had never been very careful about his comments, his associates, and his treatment of confidential documents while still king, now engaged in doing next to nothing. He was psychologically ready to move from folly to folly. Was he naïve, stupid, or just a royal scoundrel? He was naïve in his affairs of the heart, married to a twice-divorced woman who was his master and he her lackey. What about his friends? Was he naïve or stupid to continue a relationship with Charles Bedaux? Or was he using the French-American to fulfill his agenda to return to the throne under Nazi sponsorship?

The Reich had asked Karl Edward—who was Duke of Sachsen-Coburg and Gotha, Edward's cousin, and a member of the Nazi Party—to observe King Edward during his brief reign. After Karl Edward visited the king in January 1936, he told Hitler that Edward was strongly in favor of an alliance between Germany and the UK.[83]

The war started on September 1, 1939, when Germany attacked Poland. Two days later, Great Britain declared war on Germany. The Duke of Windsor, who had been named major general, reported for duty on October 2, 1939, with a British military mission. His duties were to tour the French lines and report his impressions on their state of readiness back to London. An officer accompanied Windsor and actually wrote the duke's finding report.[84]

Charles Bedaux was never very far removed from this scene, and Windsor met with him at least twice in Paris, on October 4 and November 20. Windsor's aide, Major Edward D. "Fruity" Metcalfe, said in a letter to his wife that

---

[83]   James Pool, *Who Financed Hitler?*, 93.

[84]   As king, his military rank had been marshal. The rank question was one more sore point for the Duke of Windsor.

he was concerned about Windsor's close association with Bedaux, a man whose motives he could not fathom.[85] There is a claim that Windsor used Bedaux on November 9, 1939, to inform Hitler of the French military's vulnerabilities.[86] Did this really happen? Windsor found it difficult to keep secrets, and had already been of some concern to the British cabinet. What Information was exchanged between the two men isn't known.

What we do know is that Bedaux, a U.S. citizen, traveled to Berlin via Holland during this period. Bedaux was also talking to the German embassy in Holland, whose dispatches to Berlin included information about the Duke of Windsor. On November 23, 1939, Germany made a strategic decision to attack France and the UK, to defeat Britain but not destroy it—this after Bedaux's visit to Berlin.

Meanwhile, a group that favored Germany's objectives was building around Windsor, according to Count Julius von Zech-Burkersroda, the German ambassador in The Hague, who wrote a report to State Secretary Ernst von Weizsäcker dated January 27, 1940,[87] stating that he had connections to people who could report on Windsor's

---

85   Francis Donaldson, *Edward VIII*, 376.
86   Martin Allen, *Hidden Agenda*.
87   The following is from the archive of the German Foreign Office. Item 621, p. 618, dated February 19, 1940, reports on information coming from Windsor on the Allied view of German plans for attack on Belgium. Item 648, p. 659, dated March 2, 1940, von Weizsäcker to Zech report von Ribbentrop passed information on Item 621 to Hitler. Footnote GFPD, 124/122667-68. *Akten Zur Deutschen Auswärtigen Politik* 1918-1945, Band VIII Serie D 1937-1948. Item 580, p. 561, dated January 27, 1940, report to Weizsäcker.

attitude and get messages through to him.[88] Three weeks later, von Zech-Burkersroda sent another message reporting on information coming from Windsor about the Allied view on how to react to a German attack on neutral Belgium.[89] Although no firm proof exists, Bedaux, who traveled freely and frequently to Holland, was thought to be the most likely source for these dispatches. The Abwehr thought this information was so important that it assigned Commander Traugott Andreas Richard Protze to the Hague embassy to monitor staff security.[90]

There is ample evidence that British intelligence was aware of the dangerous contacts between the gullible Duke of Windsor and the wily Charles Bedaux. Allowing those concerns to become public, however, could have meant disaster for the royal family. To this day, files on the contacts between the two men have been kept closed to public

---

[88] The number-two diplomat at the German embassy in Holland was Wolfgang zu Putlitz (1899-1975), a British agent. This being the case, it was unlikely that the British government wasn't informed about the correspondence regarding Windsor. In 1952, zu Putlitz defected to the Soviets.

[89] GMFA (German Foreign Office) Series D 1937-45, p. 618, item 618.

[90] Protze was a naval officer who had been in the Abwehr since the 1920s. He was in charge of a special counter-intelligence section responsible for detecting penetration of the Abwehr by opposition services. He had retired to Holland but was reactivated when the war broke out.

scrutiny. There is no explanation of why Britain took no direct action to eliminate or neutralize Charles Bedaux.[91]

Some claimed that the duke used Bedaux to send a message to Hitler regarding the weakness of the French defenses in the north, which led to a change in Germany's attack plans.[92] What we do know from notes kept by General Erwin von Lahousen, an important figure in the Abwehr, in that he, along with Admiral Canaris and other high-ranking officers, met with Hitler on November 23, 1939, to plan the attack on Holland and Belgium. According to von Lahousen's notes, these officers were amazed by how well Hitler was informed of the defensive situation in northern France.[93]

The German offensive was launched on May 13, 1940, and with it began yet another round of questionable behavior by the former king. After escorting his wife to the French city of Biarritz, near the Spanish frontier, Edward returned to Paris. Windsor's behavior may be explained by a common British attitude toward their French allies. American Ambassador William Bullitt's report to President Roosevelt, dated May 16, 1940, may provide insight: Three days after Germany launched its attack, Bullitt described the British as "contemptuous" of the French, and thought it was possible that to avoid the consequences of defeat,

---

[91] In February 1940 the British warned their French counterpart, the Deuxième Bureau, about doing business with Bedaux. The French ignored the warning and informed Bedaux. (Nigel West, *Guy Liddell Diaries, Vol. I,* 66.)

[92] For claims, see Martin Allen, *The Hidden Agenda.*

[93] *Institut für Zeitgeschichte* in Munich, folio 47, p. 11-16.

the British would appoint Sir Oswald Mosley to head the government.[94]

On May 27, the British military was ordered to fall back to the nearest port. Edward ignored the order, and instead joined Wallis in Biarritz. The couple then drove to Chateau de la Croë, their residence in the South of France. They left for Franco's Spain on June 19. Winston Churchill, who had become prime minister, ordered the Windsors to leave immediately for Portugal, and then return to England. But Edward refused to return unless Wallis was given the recognition of Her Royal Highness.

German intelligence, of course, was completely in the picture as agents worked closely with their Spanish counterparts. After two weeks in Spain, the Windsors went to Portugal. Herbert Claiborne Pell, the American ambassador in Lisbon, reported that the duke and duchess were indiscrete, speaking negatively of the British government. Pell advised that the Windsors not be permitted to visit the United States.[95]

The Germans were ready to undertake any kind of operation to get the duke under their control. They sent Walter Schellenberg, one of their top SS intelligence operators, to Lisbon to take charge. And, in fact, they almost succeeded. Windsor tried to remain in Lisbon, but he finally departed for the Bahamas on August 1, 1940, after

---

[94] Whether information from Windsor led to the defeat of the Franco-British forces is still not resolved. The Germans, however, did not outgun the Allies. The Western forces had "13,974 artillery pieces versus the German's 7,378, France and Britain possessed 3,524 tanks compared to the German's 2,439. The Western powers had 4,460 military aircraft versus 3,578 in the Luftwaffe." (Charles Glass, *Americans in Paris*, 212.)

[95] John H. Waller, *The Unseen War in Europe*, 168.

accepting the title of governor of the British colony. From his post in Nassau, he continued to correspond with his Spanish friend who was reporting to Spanish and German intelligence. Some would describe the duke's actions during his country's battle with Nazi Germany as on the very brink of treason.

For Edward, who was apparently most devoted to his wife, the ultimate blow to his pride was the royal family's refusal to allow his wife to be addressed as Her Royal Highness. Given his sensibilities, it wouldn't be surprising if this made him even more vulnerable to the Third Reich, and perhaps pushed him over the edge. There is no doubt that Hitler had a real interest in using Windsor as a hole card in his high-stakes poker game to disengage Great Britain from his battle to control the continent.[96]

All of these theories convened in December 1940 during a long interview with the American journalist Fulton Oursler. Windsor, as governor of the Bahamas, spoke openly of how he admired Hitler's regime, and even described the Führer as a great man. "It would be a tragic thing for the world if Hitler were overthrown," he said. "Hitler was the right and logical leader of the German people."[97] Windsor

---

[96] In the summer of 1945, British intelligence sent Officer Anthony Blunt to Schlosshotel Kronberg in Germany, the seat of the Prince of Hesse, to recover correspondence that was allegedly from Queen Victoria. There may also have been correspondence between Windsor and his cousin Hesse that embarrassed the Crown. Blunt was later discovered to be a Soviet agent. Was the correspondence passed onto KGB handlers? (See Francis Donaldson, *Edward VIII* and J. Bryan III and Charles J. V. Murphy, *The Windsor Story*.)

[97] Fulton Oursler Jr., "Secret Treason," *American Heritage*, December, 1991.

proposed that President Roosevelt act as mediator and call for peace, and he would follow by issuing a statement supporting it, bringing about a revolution and forcing peace. When Oursler met with Roosevelt and disclosed Windsor's comments, Roosevelt showed no surprise. Roosevelt had met the duke in Florida a few days before Oursler's report.

FRANCE BEFORE THE OCCUPATION

A look at the pre-war era would be helpful in order to understand the early years of Germany's occupation of France, from June 1940 to November 1942, when Charles Bedaux was involved in activities that would lead to his downfall. Events of the 1930s made life difficult for all of Europe: worldwide economic depression, fear of the spread of communism and fascism, and ongoing recovery from the First World War. But the 1930s were particularly challenging for France, which faced threats from the east by Hitler, who called for the return of lost territories. In many ways, France in the 1930s resembled Germany in the 1920s; both countries were vulnerable to extremes on the left and the right of the political spectrum that wanted to bring down democracy.

In the 1920s, Germany's Weimar Republic faced escalating conflict between the forces of the far left, the communists, and the far right, the Nazis, who were both eager to control the young democracy. When the National Socialists finally gained power in March 1933, Bedaux found new friends in high places: Georg von Stauss, Gerhardt Westrick, and so on.

France's experience was somewhat different, and one can argue that it made the country more open to the Nazi war machine of 1940, and easier to control during the subsequent occupation. France was still suffering from the horrific losses of the First World War, with more than 2.5 million casualties. Some have described the 1930s in France as a period of virtual civil war.[98] The right called for a strong central government, looking to Mussolini's Italy and Hitler's Germany as models for confronting the spread of communism from Russia, France's ally in 1914.

A radical, secret organization at the far right called *La Cagoule* (meaning "hood") was founded and financed in the 1920s by a small group of businessmen. It was ready to use violence and even assassination to achieve its objectives. François Mitterrand, the future president of France, was a member for a brief time, along with Jacques Lemaigre Dubreuil, the vegetable oil magnate who may have teamed up with Bedaux during the occupation.[99]

On February 6, 1934, about forty thousand armed right-wingers attempted to storm the Chamber of Deputies, the French parliament, leaving sixteen protestors dead

---

[98] Robert Paxton, *Vichy France*, 243.
[99] Lemaigre Dubreuil was described as "the primary fundraiser for La Cagoule" (S. Coignard and M. T. Guichard, *French Connections*, 195.)

and wounding hundreds. This galvanized the intellectual leaders who opposed France's Third Republic, and young industrial managers joined the movement, such as Pierre Pucheau, who later played critical roles in Vichy.[100]

The left gained power in the May 3, 1936, general election. The victorious socialists joined with the communists for the first time, forming the Popular Front government. The immediate problem the new government faced was the widespread strikes that were crippling the economy. Leon Blum, the new (and first) socialist premier, called a meeting between labor unions and employer associations. Charles Bedaux was also invited to participate, to settle the disputes. Labor won wage increases, and Bedaux received his first *Légion d'honneur* for contributing to what became known as the Matignon Agreements. But Bedaux's participation is a puzzle. Earlier that year, he had spent six weeks visiting the USSR, and certainly wasn't considered a friend of labor, with his "speed-up king" title. Some claim that Maurice Thorez, the communist labor leader, invited Bedaux.[101]

For many on France's far right, "better Hitler than Blum" was an acceptable solution to the labor management problem. They saw the new Germany as an effective barrier to the spread of communism from the Soviet Union. During the Weimar era, longtime enemies Germany and France had begun reconciling by encouraging contacts at the economic, social, and cultural levels. Veterans groups and others founded organizations on both sides of the

---

[100] Pucheau served the Vichy government as minister of the interior, where he sanctioned the severe reprisals carried out by the Nazi occupiers. He was tried for treason and executed by the Free French Forces in Casablanca in March 1944.

[101] Jim Christy, *The Price of Power*, 136.

border with reconciliation as their goal. Once Hitler came to power, however, these activities took a different form.

The National Socialists didn't trust the professional diplomats in the German foreign affairs ministry, and so they established the *Büro Ribbentrop* (Ribbentrop Bureau), a parallel operation headed by the former champagne salesman Joachim von Ribbentrop, who was given the title Special Ambassador. Von Ribbentrop received the assignment because of his business experience with Britain and France, and his fluency in both languages. Büro Ribbentrop employees were to establish relationships with groups in France and Great Britain that could be useful to the Nazis. Two early Büro Ribbentrop members were Otto Abetz and Julius Westrick, both important players in Charles Bedaux's life.

Otto Abetz, born in 1913, first worked as an art teacher in the German state of Baden. Fascinated by French culture, he became active in cross-border youth movements during the Weimar era. In 1934, as a member of the Büro Ribbentrop, the Hitler *Jungvolk* (Hitler Youth) organization assigned Abetz with developing links to French youth groups. Abetz was married to a French woman, Suzanne Sidonie, and he joined the SS paramilitary group in 1935 and the Nazi Party in 1937. Some have called Abetz's pre-war French activities the "Charm Offensive."[102] In fact, Abetz was proud to represent the so-called soft side of Germany's policy, which envisioned France as a satellite of the Third Reich—exploited yet integrated in the New Order, and contributing to the fight against Bolshevism.

---

[102] Roland Ray, *Annaeherung*.

The *Deutsch-Französische Gesellschaft* (German-French Association, or DFG), organized by a group of writers and academics in the 1920s and closed down in 1933, was a vehicle to achieve this goal. It was re-launched on October 25, 1935, at a gala event in which many of Germany's elite attended. On November 22, 1935, the French counterpart, *Comité France-Allemagne* (CFA), was founded.

Georg von Stauss, honorary chairman of the DFG, was vice president of the Reichstag and supervisory board member of Deutsche Bank. Otto Abetz and Julius Westrick were assigned to keep tabs on the CFA and to liaison with the DFG. The CFA, now incarnated, lobbied to further Nazi goals. It was during this period, December 1935, that Julius Westrick accompanied Georg von Stauss to Bedaux's Chateau de Candé, and the collaboration between the German banker and the renowned management consultant began.

As Germany's aggressive stance toward its neighbors became more apparent—the March 1938 *Anschluss* (incorporation) of Austria into the Third Reich and the Sudeten crisis with Czechoslovakia later that year—CFA membership became less effective for the Nazis. Some members were now wary of their neighbor's true intentions toward France. Still, when the occupation came in 1940, Abetz knew where to look for instant and eager collaboration.

During July 1939, the French press was full of stories about the threat of war and the fear that hundreds of

German spies were in their midst. The press named Otto Abetz, among others. The French government ordered Abetz to leave France—it knew about Abetz's role in influencing public opinion by questioning the trustworthiness of the British in the looming crisis between Poland and the Reich.

In late August, Bedaux, von Stauss, and Abetz flew from Berlin to Salzburg to meet with von Ribbentrop, who wanted to learn about Bedaux's ideas about replacing the gold standard with his "unit of work."[103] During this meeting, Hitler ordered von Ribbentrop to proceed to Moscow to negotiate the German-Soviet Non-Aggression Pact, which freed up the Reich to attack Poland.

On his return to Berlin, Bedaux met with Hjalmar Schacht, president of the Reichsbank—who at the moment was out of favor with Hitler—to discuss the "unit of work" idea with him. Schacht, of course, thought it was crazy, the kind of hare-brained proposal that only von Ribbentrop would entertain.

Germany invaded Poland on September 1. France and Great Britain, treaty-bound to support Poland, declared war on Germany. The world was introduced to Blitzkrieg, the rapid advance of Germany's mechanized army against the Poles, who still rode to battle on horseback. After seventeen days, the Poland campaign was over, and Poland was divided between the Reich and the USSR as part of the German-Soviet Non-Aggression Pact.

---

[103] The three men wanted von Ribbentrop to support Bedaux's reentry into the German market. It was then that Foreign Minister von Ribbentrop recommended that Bedaux hire Gerhardt Westrick as his attorney.

Hitler believed that a settlement with the Western Allies was possible, and there were men in high places in both countries that favored this. To Hitler, Germany's treaty with the Soviets was only a strategy to gain time. His real goal was to obtain Lebensraum by expanding to the east. (If only the West would cooperate!) But there was no peace negotiation, and the period known as the "phony war" began.

When the war began, Bedaux offered his company's services to Raoul Dautry, the French minister for armaments production, who quickly accepted the offer. Dautry asked Bedaux to survey the aircraft and weapons production industries. It seems odd that Bedaux was given this assignment in light of his frequent visits to Germany, which must have been known to French counter-intelligence.

In March 1940, Dautry asked Bedaux to travel to Spain, where Marshal Philippe Pétain was the French ambassador, to obtain three hundred thousand tons of Spanish steel for France's weapons production.[104] Bedaux found that Spain had sufficient iron ore and mill capacity, but not enough coal to produce the steel. He then traveled to Morocco, where he surveyed the Kenadsa coal mines and announced that he could increase production four-fold, more than enough to supply Spain's steel industry.[105] While in Spain, he also did contract work for Portugal's Salazar government.

Bedaux returned to Paris on June 7, with hardly enough time to execute his Kenadsa plan before the French military collapse. He received his second Légion d'honneur for his

---

[104] Pétain had been appointed to this position in March 1939, following General Franco's nationalist victory.

[105] Kenadsa coal mines were in southern Algeria, a disputed area with Morocco.

contribution to the French war effort.[106] But Bedaux was not only helping France—at the war's outbreak he offered Chateau de Candé as a retreat for the American embassy, which they gratefully accepted. Some embassy personnel moved to the Chateau, and by June 1940 it housed about five hundred refugees.

We know that on November 8 Hitler left the traditional Munich party rally early—thereby missing an attempt on his life—for an important meeting the next day in Berlin. (Could this have been with Bedaux?) Soon after, Hitler ordered a new plan to attack France, a plan developed by General Manstein that was later known as the Manstein Plan.

---

[106] Although they had been warned about doing business with Bedaux. (Nigel West, *Guy Liddell Diaries, Vol. I*, 66.)

THE FALL OF FRANCE—
AND BEDAUX

On June 14, 1940, German troops marched into Paris, signaling the fall of France. A few days later, an armistice was signed in Compiègne, inside the same railroad car in which Germany had surrendered in November 1918. The government in Bordeaux decided not to seek a so-called Holland Solution, in which they would have retreated to North Africa and carried on the fight from there, as the Dutch had done when Queen Wilhelmina departed for Great Britain. The premier, Paul Reynaud, favored this, but the Army under command of General Maxime Weygand refused.[107]

France, with a population of 42 million, was divided into an occupied zone under the control of the German military. Roughly two-thirds of France was inside the zone: 23 million people living in Paris and 21,000 other cities, towns, and villages in forty-nine of the country's eighty-seven departments. The zone's demarcation line separated it from Vichy France. It ran north-west from Geneva and the Swiss border to Dole; west through Chateau-sur-Saône, Moulins and Vierzon; and southeast of Tours, Poitiers and Angoulême, reaching the Spanish frontier near Saint-Jean-Pied-de-Port, at the foot of the Pass de Roncesvalles.[108] Bedaux's Chateau de Candé was not far from Tours, only thirteen kilometers or eight miles. The German occupation authority in Belgium controlled two French departments in the north, Pas-de-Calais and Nord, due to their close economic links with the area.

A new government for the rest of the country—and France's vast overseas empire—was established in the sleepy spa town of Vichy. At its head was the hero of Verdun, eighty-four-year-old Marshal Philippe Pétain. Before the war, Pétain had been the French ambassador to Franco Spain, and had been the minister of war in the cabinet that agreed to sign the armistice. Pierre Laval, fifty-seven years

---

[107] Maxime Weygand (1867-1965) served briefly as defense minister under Pétain in Vichy, then was commander of French forces in African colonies.

[108] Ian Ousby, *Occupation*, 67.

old, a well-known and clever pre-war politician, was vice president.[109]

Map credit: Thomas Fontaine, Chronology of Repression and Persecution in Occupied France, 1940-44, Online Encyclopedia of Mass Violence, [online], published November 19, 2007, accessed January 25, 2011, URL: http://www.massviolence. org/Chronology-of-Repression-and-Persecution-in-Occupied-France, ISSN 1961-9898

---

[109] Laval's only child, Jose, was married to Comte René de Chambrun, a descendant of Marquis de Lafayette, the French hero of the American Revolution. René de Chambrun (1906-2002), whose mother was an American, Clara Longworth, married Laval's daughter in 1935. A dominant international lawyer, he was a staunch advocate for his father-in-law, who was tried and executed in October 1945.

Pétain and Laval were as different as can be. Pétain had been the hero of Verdun, the devastating battle of the First World War. Neat in appearance and a non-smoker, he believed his role was to be savior of France. Laval was a shrewd politician who had been in various governments in the 1920s and early '30s. Having become rich after having come from humble circumstances,[110] he dressed sloppily, chain smoked, and saw his role as deal-cutter with the Nazis to make France a satellite in the New Europe.[111]

As early as July 1940, Laval met with Otto Abetz, now the German ambassador in Paris, and offered to join the Reich against Great Britain. (And why not pick up pieces of Britain's overseas empire to compensate for Europe's losses?) Admiral Darlan, who had replaced Laval in 1941, again put this idea forward when he proposed a joint French-German attack on the British colonies in Africa. Fortunately for the history of France, Hitler was more interested in revenge than alliance; people like Abetz were never permitted to go beyond listening to these proposals.[112]

Many of the leading personalities in the Vichy government came from the private Worms Bank, which was founded in the nineteenth century by a Jewish family originally from Frankfurt, Germany. The bank worked with Great Britain during the pre-war years, but during the war

---

[110] He made his money by acquiring ownership of Radio-Lyon and the *Lyon-Republican* newspaper in 1928.

[111] Robert Paxton, *Vichy France*, 66.

[112] On the one occasion, April 1941, when Vichy allowed its colony Syria to be used as a re-supply base in support of the attempted putsch, led by Rashid Ali-Al-Gailani (who was a German puppet) against the British in Iraq, Syria was lost to the Free French of Charles De Gaulle.

it became known as a political bank with close ties to Vichy and the German conquerors.

Many leaders of Vichy also thought that France should clean its slate of the 1920s and '30s decadence, and return to its roots for salvation. Their idealized world was one in which church and state were one, and the people once again were small farmers and artisans who no longer engaged in the American style of mass production. During the pre-war years a number of prominent French intellectuals had been advocating the same line in writing and discourse.

The Vichy government's number-one goal was to protect France's overseas empire and to expand it at Britain's expense. Charles Bedaux's know-how, experience, and ambition made him appear to be an attractive agent to achieve these objectives. Foreign embassies, including that of the United States, soon set up shop in the sleepy spa town. Vichy became a center of intrigue.

In the meantime, Germany's plan to control and exploit the occupation zone was quickly shaping up. Otto Abetz, who became ambassador in August 1940, was again operating on the Rue de Ville. Rudolf Schleier, a businessman who headed the Nazi Party in France before the war, assisted Abetz. His duties also included "watching over Abetz," and later in the war, von Ribbentrop assigned Schleier to "prepare anti-Jewish drives abroad."[113] Schleier was described as the "uncompromising party man" in the embassy.[114]

---

[113] Schleier had been posted to the ministry as head of personnel in the department of information. (Marie Vassitchikov, *Berlin Diaries 1940-1945*, 178.)

[114] Rudolf Schleier (1899-1956) (David Price Jones, *Paris in the Third Reich*, 235.)

Ernst Achenbach, thirty-one years old, was the ranking professional diplomat, having served at the embassy in the pre-war years.[115] Married to an American, he was always a little suspect in some circles. After the war, Achenbach was elected to the Bundestag and the European parliament as a member of the centrist Free Democratic Party (FDP). He resigned after being linked to the transport of French Jews "to the east"—a euphemism for death camps.

Then there was Professor Friedrich Grimm, the well-known defense lawyer who was a lecturer and propagandist in the pre-war years. At the embassy, he did much of the same thing.[116]

Last but not least, Julius Westrick was also assigned to the embassy. Bedaux's lawyer Gerhardt Westrick's younger brother, Julius Westrick's title was now *Legationsrat*, or counselor to a legation. Westrick had worked in France during the pre-war years on assignment with the Büro Ribbentrop, developing relationships with French contacts that could be helpful to the Reich. In November 1935, he and Abetz worked to re-establish a Comité France-Allemagne.[117] Also in 1935, Westrick accompanied von Stauss of Deutsche Bank on von Stauss's first visit to Bedaux's Chateau de Candé. Now Westrick's mission was to develop relations with and monitor the activities of French rightist groups that were eager to work with the occupation.

Germany invaded Russia on June 22, 1941, a year to the day after the French-German armistice was signed. Westrick organized a conference at the Hotel Majestic

---

[115] Ernst Achenbach (1909-1991)

[116] Grimm's reports on France are on file at Germany's national archive in Koblenz. The reports show that even after the war he continued to be an effective Nazi defender.

[117] Roland Ray, *Annäherung*, 173.

for the leadership of these French rightist groups, and the *Légion des Volontaires Francais* (LVF) was launched. The LVF sent its men to the Russian Front to battle communism with their friends from other occupied countries.[118] As Bedaux's story developed, Gerhard Westrick from time to time called upon Julius Westrick's services. Later in the war, as the German forces were forced to retreat from France, Julius helped leading French collaborationists find refuge in Germany.

The military side of the occupation was divided into two staffs: the administration staff under General Werner Best, and the economic staff under General Elmar Michel.[119] General Franz Albrecht Medicus, who reported to General Michel, soon developed a close relationship with Bedaux.

Until the Allies invaded North Africa in November 1942, the Germans never had more than thirty thousand troops to keep the peace in the occupied zone—a force only twice the size of the Paris police force.

Even during this "quiet" period, however, all was not sweetness and light. The two departments in the north that the German military administration in Belgium controlled, Nord and Pas-de-Calais, were important coal mining centers. The Bedaux method was introduced to increase worker productivity, but in response, the miners went on

---

[118] Westrick had been a pilot during the First World War. He was shot down by Pierre Constantini, who became an important figure in the LVF. The two became friends in the inter-war years. (J. G. Shields, "Charlemagne's Crusaders," 80.)

[119] Before the war, Michel had the rank of *Ministerialdirektor* in the Ministry of Economic Affairs. After the war, he served in the Erhard Ministry of Economic Affairs. Upon retirement, he became CEO of the Salamander Shoe Company.

strike. The strike lasted from May 27 to June 6, 1941, but was brutally repressed.[120]

In addition, the military's economic administration functioned to exploit France's resources and rid the French economy of Jewish participation, a policy called *Entjudung*. Michel sent a notice to all field officers ordering them to get French officials to participate in Entjudung, which made them share the responsibility.[121] Meanwhile, Bedaux's friend, Dr. Medicus, was eminently qualified to lead Entjudung.

General Franz Albrecht Medicus, born in 1890, was a lawyer with a classical education, fluent in Latin and Greek, who spent leisure time photographing French cathedrals and churches. (His photographs are still available in book form.) Indeed, Dr. Medicus was a solid civil servant in the pre-war Ministry of the Interior, with the rank of *Ministerialdirigent*, or ministerial counsellor. His real claim to fame was co-authoring the infamous 1935 Nuremberg Laws, which restricted the activities of Germany's Jewish citizens.[122]

Bedaux and Medicus met in September 1940 at a dinner party at the home of Andre Dubonnet (of the Dubonnet drink family), and became fast friends. Their relationship was intriguing. Medicus became a frequent weekend guest at Chateau de Candé. We have to remember that although Bedaux was an active collaborator and may have been a

---

[120]   Robert Paxton, *Vichy France*, 376.

[121]   David Price Jones, *Paris in the Third Reich*, 82.

[122]   Medicus was born in 1890 in Straßburg and died in 1967 in Wiesbaden. In 1933 he joined the SS as an *Oberregierungsrat* in the Ministry of the Interior. In 1934 he was promoted to *Ministerialdirigent* and was a lecturer at the Deutsche Hochschule für Politik, which in 1937 was controlled by Josef Göbbels. Medicus joined the Nazi Party in 1937.

German agent as long ago as the First World War, from time to time he had problems with the German occupation bureaucracy. Medicus joined the Westricks, Abetz, and von Stauss in the German circle of contacts who supported Bedaux's ambitions. Medicus was also a welcome guest in collaborationist upper-crust society circles—he attended a fancy dress ball in December 1940 at Baron Johnny Empain's Chateau de Bouffémont. Empain was chairman of the Paris Métro.

Medicus helped loot art treasures in Paris when he accompanied Hermann Göring for that purpose on February 4, 1941. On November 14, 1942, after the Allies landed in North Africa, Medicus was reassigned to General Alexander von Neubronn's staff. Von Neubronn was the Vichy representative of the senior commander in the west, Field Marshal Gerd von Rundstedt.[123]

Medicus continued to be a loyal servant of the Reich, and was not involved in the plot against Hitler on July 20, 1944. He was captured at the end of the hostilities, and he wrote a complaint with detailed statistics about the conditions in an American Army screening camp in the Stuttgart area, where prisoners were held while being checked for war crimes. In his report, Medicus compared the camp to a concentration camp. In addition, Medicus's daughter Dorothee worked as Fern Bedaux's social secretary for several years after the war.[124]

---

[123] In 1944, von Rundstedt was in command of the military administration in occupied Greece.

[124] A document written by Medicus in late October of 1943 (MA 677, on file at the *Institut für Zeitgeschichte* in Munich) explains *Entjudung*, the elimination of the Jews from the French economy.

Now that we've identified some key players in the French and German administrations with whom Bedaux was involved, we ask this: What was the renowned consultant doing during June 1940 and November 1942? Well, he was very busy. As always, he was using his creativity and his awesome ability to sell ideas to influence decision-makers in the French and German administrations. But he also had bureaucratic obstacles to overcome. The seat of Bedaux International was in Holland, and by that point, the German military in Brussels—completely separate from the administration in Paris—occupied and controlled Holland. Internationale Bedaux MIJN.V. in Amsterdam was a registered Dutch company, and was confiscated as enemy property. Karl Gartner, a German commissioner who had been a Bedaux engineer, was appointed to oversee operations, but Gartner was not Bedaux's favorite. With Gerhard Westrick's help in Berlin, Bedaux replaced Gartner with Heinrich Schlichtwein, his German partner. Bedaux considered Schlichtwein to be better qualified to use the Bedaux System, and imagined that he would be able to expand the business.

To change commissioners, Westrick had to convince Frederich-Franz Sperl, the *Reichskommissar* for enemy property, of Bedaux's importance to the Nazi war effort. Westrick argued that the Reich would be interested in anything that improved worker productivity.[125]

The Japanese attacked Pearl Harbor on December 7, 1941. Germany was Japan's ally (the Tripartite Pact of September 20, 1940, was signed by Japan, Italy, and Germany) and Hitler declared war on the United States

---

[125]   Bundesarchiv Koblenz, Bestand 1200, Band 1043. *Nachlass Gerhard Alois Westrick.*

on December 11, 1941. Charles and Fern Bedaux, who were American citizens, had ignored the earlier request by the United States to leave occupied Europe. Germany considered them enemy aliens, and the Gestapo interned them until the Abwehr intervened, releasing them. Bedaux, fearing that Bedaux International in Amsterdam would be confiscated, traveled to Holland to move the company files to Paris in March 1942, with the assistance of Medicus and the Abwehr. An Abwehr officer, Captain von Sertz, accompanied him. Von Sertz was on the staff of *Fregattenkapitän* Erich Pheiffer, head of Abwehr I, which was responsible for foreign intelligence.

Pheiffer was considered one of the best agent handlers in the service. He had previously been assigned to the Bremen office, which specialized in espionage against the United States. Dr. Nikolas Bensmann, a patent attorney working for the Texas Oil Company, was one of Pheiffer's key operatives, so Pheiffer was considered ideally qualified to handle a high-level source like Charles Bedaux.[126] Accompanied to Holland by an Abwehr captain, Bedaux moved around freely. Bedaux was able to retrieve his files and also brought his loyal manageress, Alessandra Ter Hart, a Jewess, back with him to Paris.

Once the occupation began, Bedaux had been able to obtain, with Otto Abetz's help, WH automobile license plates that were reserved for high command and favored civilians. So Bedaux was able to travel around Paris at will, even though there were only about seven thousand private

---

[126] Bensmann, being fluent in English, organized an intelligence operation within the Texas Oil Company. He continued to be involved with the Bedaux case.

cars in the city.[127] French civilians and uniformed Germans staffed his offices in Avenue Friedland. In addition to having worldwide experience, he had contacts in the German Embassy, in the Abwehr, in French business circles, and in Vichy.

Charles Eugène Bedaux was ready to do business.

---

[127]   David Price Jones, *Paris in the Third Reich*, 99.

Emil Georg von Stauss (1877-1942) - Member of the supervisory board of the Deutsche Bank, Member of the Reichstag for the Deutsche Volkspartei and appointed vice-president of that organization by Hermann Göring. Met Charles Bedaux in 1935 and became his unofficial advisor.

Charles and Fern Bedaux in Paris, September 28th, 1942, shortly after their release from being caught in a German sweep of foreigners. Fern, a native of Grand Rapids, Michigan, was his second wife.

The Duke of Windsor and Mrs. Simpson on their wedding day, June 3, 1937 at the Chateau de Cande of Charles Bedaux.

Duke and Duchess of Windsor with Fern and Charles Bedaux, September 1937 at the Bedaux estate in Hungary where plans for the visit to Germany and the United States were made.

The Duke and Duchess of Windsor with Adolf Hitler in October 1937 on their visit to Germany, arranged by Charles Bedaux

General Franz Albrecht Medicus (1890-1967)- 1942 in Paris assigned to the German occupation administration. A friend of Charles Bedaux, he served in the Third Reich Ministry of the Interior where he was co-author of the 1935 Nuremburg Laws restricting the activities of Germany's Jewish citizens.

THE ABADAM PROJECT

For modern armies on the move, there is one critical resource without which aggressive action is impossible: oil. Pre-war Germany had agreements with Romania, the major supplier in Europe, some of which were negotiated by Georg von Stauss of Deutsche Bank. For much of his career, von Stauss had specialized in the bank's oil interests.[128]

The USSR had important oil fields in the Baku area, and they would be an objective for Germany's attack that was launched in June 1941. But the most important known oil deposits outside the United States were in Iran and Iraq, where the British were well established. One of Bedaux's major clients was the Anglo-Iranian Oil Company, whose refinery at Abadan was probably the largest in the world. Bedaux's knowledge of this key installation made him destined to play a key role in the Third Reich's war plans for the region.

To understand how we got from "there to here," it helps to take a brief look at the history of the area. The Near East, now known as the Middle East, had long been part of the

---

[128] Lothar Gall, *The Deutsche Bank*, 141.

Ottoman Empire, which by the nineteenth century was in such decline that it was called the "sick man of Europe." Thus began a competition among the great powers of Europe—Great Britain, France, Austria-Hungary, Russia, and, somewhat later, Germany—to make economic and political gains in the area. In 1878, Chancellor Otto von Bismark of Germany sponsored the conference that resulted in the Treaty of Berlin, which slowed Russia's advance in the Ottoman Empire. Sultan Abdul Hamid II perceived the Germans to be the protectors of the Turks, and invited German officers to help build a modern army and military academy.[129] German investment and economic development soon followed.

In 1888, Deutsche Bank headed a syndicate that signed a 99-year concession to operate the Haidar-Pasha-Ismid Railway. From this a plan evolved to link Berlin with Baghdad by rail, on which goods were to be transported duty-free.[130] The British, of course, didn't ignore this development. Through their leverage in the form of Turkish bonds that were in danger of defaulting, the British managed to be appointed to the railroad board in 1913. Germany also agreed not to extend the railroad beyond Basra in Iraq.[131]

---

[129] Abdul Hamid II (1842-1918) had lost a war with czarist Russia in 1877-78. He was forced to sign the Treaty of San Stefano, which Bismarck revised favorably for the Ottomans in the Treaty of Berlin.

[130] The link to Baghdad was completed in 1940. (Wolfgang Schwanitz, *Germany and the Middle East*, 3.)

[131] As a naval lieutenant in 1913, Admiral Canaris had been assigned to observe the progress being made on the railroad construction in Anatolia. (Heinz Höhne, *Canaris*, 15.)

Hundreds of German military, technical, and engineering personnel soon followed.[132]

When the First World War began in August 1914, Germany and Turkey were allies in the Central Powers pact, and were on the losing side. But although Germany's banks, industries, and military had lost to the British and French, Germany had left a positive image behind in the Middle East. The League of Nations granted mandates to the British over Iraq and to the French over Syria and Lebanon. Kemal Atatürk, the "strong man" of Turkey, who had served as a general and had worked closely with German officers in the First World War, looked favorably upon economic and cultural cooperation with his former allies.[133]

German universities were leaders in engineering and the sciences, and were magnets for students from the Middle East. In 1939, thousands of German business people, technical personnel, and tourists were deployed from Turkey and eastward to India. Among them were representatives of the Nazi Party and agents of the Abwehr. The area was, to a large extent, dominated by the British and, to a lesser extent, French economic investment. Germany already had plans for the control and conquest of the territory of Afghanistan and Persia during the First World War, as a part of Kaiser Wilhelm II's ambition to make the Reich a world power.

In 1914, Max von Oppenheim (1860-1946), a German archaeologist and Middle East specialist, succeeded in getting

---

[132] My father-in-law surveyed the Anatolian region on horseback in 1908, when he was a young engineer working for Philip Holzmann, Germany's largest construction company at the time.

[133] Atatürk came to power in 1923 after defeating the sultan's forces; the sultan had invited the British and Americans into Turkey. Atatürk died in 1938.

the Ottoman ruler to call for a jihad by the Arabs in the British and French colonies.[134] In 1940, the eighty-year-old von Oppenheim presented a plan to the Ribbentrop foreign ministry for the German takeover of the Arab countries of the Middle East. However, it was not implemented due to Hitler's priority: planning the attack on the USSR.

In 1915-16, Oskar Ritter von Niedermayer (1885-1948) led an Indo-German-Turkish mission to Kabul in Afghanistan, where he organized Arab revolts in British and French occupied territories. As a student of the renowned geopolitical professor Albert Haushofer, von Niedermayer had specialized in Iran's geography. In the Second World War, von Niedermayer commanded a unit of volunteers from the Caucasus and Middle East. This so-called East Legion was to be part of a pincers attack, a military maneuver, from Egypt and the Caucasus colonies[135] in the Middle East, if the Rommel and the Russian campaigns had succeeded.[136]

At the beginning of World War Two, the Abwehr's priorities were not targets in the Middle East, although agents were deployed in key locations. The German-Soviet Pact of 1939 seemed to ensure a supply of oil from that area. From 1939 to early 1940, Germany considered the French army in Syria, made up of 125,000-150,000 men under the

---

[134] Oppenheim was based in Constantinople (Istanbul), where he was in charge of the intelligence bureau for the east.

[135] There were thirty thousand Germans in the Ottoman's army during the First World War. Germany's General Hans von Seekt was the last chief of staff of the Ottoman Army. (Wolfgang Schwanitz, *Germany and the Middle East,* 9.)

[136] The Nazis imprisoned Niedermayer in 1944. Liberated by the U.S. Army in 1945, he then chose to travel to the Soviet occupied territory, where he was sentenced to twenty-five years. He died in 1948.

command of General Maxine Weygand, a potential threat to the USSR's Baku oil fields. With this situation in mind, in March 1940 Captain Paul Leverkühn, a reserve Abwehr officer, was assigned under cover of consul in Tabriz, Iran, to do a reconnaissance of the area for possible military operations. Leverkühn was the last surviving officer of the Scheubner-Richter expedition that had operated in the same area during the winter of 1915-1916.[137]

As Leverkühn described it, the Abwehr once again became interested in his reconnaissance as the German army advanced in the Caucasus in late 1941, and an operation against the Mosul oil field and the Abadan refinery seemed possible.[138]

Even earlier, the Abwehr was being prompted to harass the British in the region. Soon after the war started, *Oberregierungsrat* Wohrl, the Abwehr's man in Kabul, Afghanistan, proposed that a coup be launched to reinstate pro-German King Amanullah, who had been out of office since 1929 and considered strongly anti-British.[139]

Germany had established weekly air service between Kabul and Berlin in 1938, the first of its kind. The Organization Todt made plans and supervised major

---

[137] He was later assigned to a lead position in the Abwehr operation in Turkey. Leverkühn, an international lawyer, also served in the post-war German parliament.

[138] Paul Leverkühn, *German Military Intelligence,* 8.

[139] On February 17, 1941, Hitler ordered a plan for Afghanistan to attack India, to be launched by captured Indian troops who were ready to join the Free India movement headed by Subhas Chandra Bose. (Klaus Hildebrand, *The Foreign Policy,* 109, and Martin Kitchen, *A Military History of Germany,* 82-316.)

infrastructure projects.[140] German officers trained and equipped the Afghan army. German trade with Afghanistan increased ten-fold in the two years before the war. By 1940, Germany was described as Afghanistan's most important friend.[141]

The German plan was to use Afghanistan as a base to encourage problems for the British in India in the event of a war. But the real objective of the Reich was to gain access to the Middle East oil fields.

By 1939, Iraq was one of the major oil producers in the Middle East, with a young new king, three-year-old Faisal II, and a British-mandated country. Iraq and Britain had signed a twenty-five year alliance treaty in 1930, and under the treaty's terms, Iraq was obligated to support Britain in the event of war. In 1934, the export of oil began and the Iraq Petroleum Company, a British-controlled enterprise, played a dominant role in Iraq's economy.

Franz von Papen, the man who had helped Hitler gain power and who had served as vice-chancellor, was Germany's ambassador in Turkey during the war. One of

---

[140] Operation Todt, or OT, named after its founder Dr. Fritz Todt, was responsible for major engineering and construction projects in Germany during the pre-war years, and in occupied territories during WWII.

[141] By 1939, the Germans in Afghanistan outnumbered the British ten to one. (Wolfgang Schwanitz, *Germany and the Middle East*, 60, 78.)

his missions was to get Turkey to support the Germany's takeover of Iraq's oil resources.[142]

In November 1940, Kurt Weigelt, a Deutsche Bank director, asked von Papen to "initiate negotiations with the Iraqi government for the return of crude oil concessions."[143]

Dr. Fritz Grobba, an expert on the Middle East, also became a strong advocate for supporting a revolt against the British. Grobba had served in the Middle East in the First World War, married a Syrian girl, converted to Islam, and had been a German ambassador in Baghdad. He had arranged assignments for Iraqi officers to attend German maneuvers and for German officers to be stationed in Iraq as trainers. Seven coup attempts occurred between 1936 and 1941. Under pressure from the Reich's Ministry of Foreign Affairs, the *Oberkommando der Wehrmacht* (OKW) agreed to support a new coup attempt by Rashid Ali al-Gailani, the former pro-German prime minister who wanted to rid Iraq of the British.

Al-Gailani received German support through Syria, a mandate of France, and the coup was launched on April 3, 1941. In May 1941, Admiral Darlan, the Vichy France premier, signed the Paris Protocols, which gave Germany use of Syrian airfields to support the revolt. The agreement also allowed Germany the use of submarine bases in Bizerte, a Tunisian port, to support General Rommel's Afrikakorps and, at some point in the future, Dakar in Senegal. The

---

[142] Turkey and Germany signed a friendship pact on June 18, 1941, a few days before the invasion of the USSR. Von Papen's aim was to make Turkey a satellite of Nazi Germany. (Wolfgang Schwanitz, *Germany and the Middle East*, 183, 188.)

[143] Ibid., 194.

coup managed to oust the pro-British regent Emir Abd al-Ilah, but it was defeated in June 1941. The consequence? Vichy lost Syria to Charles de Gaulle's Free French Forces. Al-Gailani fled to Teheran, accompanied by the Grand Mufti of Jerusalem, and from there the two were brought to Berlin, where they worked for the Nazi propaganda machine.[144]

Had the coup succeeded, German and Italian interests would have controlled Iraq Petroleum Company. Much of the wealth of the British Empire was either located in the Middle East or required passage through the area. From the Abwehr's perspective, neutralizing this area or making it less bountiful for the British was an important target in peacetime and even more so when the war began in September 1939. German agents and operations were active in Afghanistan and Iraq. Iran, however, the major oil producer with the world's biggest refinery, Abadan, was high on the priority list. According to C. Skring, the British consul in Teheran, who quoted Ambassador Sir Reader Bullard: "Persia and Hitler Germany were complementary to one another." The Iranians had raw materials, foodstuffs to offer in trade for manufactured products from Germany. In 1940-41 Iran, imports from Germany were 47.2 percent of total imports and exports to Germany made up 42.9 percent of Iran's total exports.[145]

Commerce became a political asset for Germany. Reza Shah Pahlavi, interested in industrializing Iran, encouraged

---

[144] Al-Gailani spent the post-war years in exile in Saudi Arabia. In 1956 he announced his support of Gamal Abdel Nasser, the dictator of Egypt, in his efforts to topple the Iraqi regime. Al-Gailani was one of the founders of the Moslem Brotherhood.

[145] Wolfgang Schwanitz, *Germany and the Middle East,* 169.

the Germans to build factories and bring specialists to train his people. Two to three thousand Germans were based in Iran in July 1941, and another four thousand were there on short-term visas.[146] [147] In the 1930s, German diplomats encouraged Reza Shah to change his country's name from Persia to Iran. The Reich's racist theorists claimed, through their pseudo-science, that Indo-Aryan was the proper way to describe the ancient civilizations of Mesopotamia. The British and Soviets occupied Iran in August 1941 and forced Reza Shah into exile. His son, Mohammad Reza Pahlavi, replaced him.

Enter Charles Eugène Bedaux, the world-renowned consultant. He was well traveled, well connected and, we shall see, eager to prove his worth to the only people he could still do business with, Hitler Germany. The Anglo-Iranian Oil Company was a Bedaux client and a high priority for the Abwehr. The company was founded in Iran in 1908 following the discovery of a major oil field, and it received a sixty-year concession on very favorable terms.

Bedaux had visited the installations in Iran several times, beginning in 1935 and most recently in 1938. He reported to the company chairman, Lord Cadman, on improving the operating efficiency of the Abadan refinery, the largest in the world.

During the war years Iran was the major oil producer in the Middle East, producing in 1943 about 75 million

---

[146] During the First World War, hundreds of German and Austrian POWs had escaped from Russian camps in the Tashkent area and had reached Teheran.

[147] Germany had long been fascinated with the field of Arabic studies. The University of Heidelberg offered courses on the subject in 1609. Yale was the first university to do so in the United States, in 1841.

barrels of the region's 121 million barrels. Iraq was number two with 25 million barrels. Abadan gave the British 85 percent of the region's refining capacity.

Abadan is located in the Khuzestan area of Iran, on an island along the eastern bank of the Shatt Al-Arab River. The island is 42 miles (68 km) long, and varies in width from 2 to 12 miles (3 to 19 km).[148] The island is 33 miles (53 km) from the Persian Gulf, along Iran's border with Iraq.

The Abadan refinery began operations in 1913 and one year later, shortly before the start of the First World War, began to supply the British Navy, whose fleet was being converted from coal to oil. At the urging of Winston Churchill, who was First Lord of the Admirality, the company was partly nationalized in 1913 to ensure the continuing supply of oil to the British Navy. The British government became a major shareholder.

During the Second World War, Abadan became a key supplier of aviation fuel for the Royal Air Force (RAF). Shortly before the war, on his last visit with Lord Cadman, Bedaux may well have discussed the vulnerability of Abadan to aerial attack. Such a conversation can't be confirmed, but what is beyond dispute is that in the first year of the war, the Italians bombed the British refinery in Haifa, Palestine. The success of this operation may have encouraged the

---

[148] In 1951 Dr. Mohammad Mossadegh became prime minister of Iran and nationalized the Anglo-Iranian Oil Company. In a 1953 coup, the Mossadegh government was ousted and the ownership returned to the old shareholders. The company was renamed British Petroleum. Abadan in 1950 had a throughput capacity of 25 million tons a year. During the 1980 Iran-Iraq war, Abadan was almost captured in a surprise attack launched by Iraq's Saddam Hussein.

development of Bedaux's plan to protect and the save the Abadan refinery from a similar fate.

The Abwehr was certain that if Abadan was attacked and in danger of being captured, the British would destroy the facilities. The Abwehr was assigned to develop a plan to prevent such destruction.[149] Bedaux's plan was described as the *système d'ensablement*, the sanding-up technique.[150] The idea was to sabotage the pipelines before the British could do so, but in a way that would allow for their fast recovery. Bedaux's idea was to fill the well borings and pipelines not with desert sand but with fluid sand, which came from sandstone readily available in the area. Using this method, it would take three days to fill the pipelines and only two days to clear them.

In 1941 Bedaux began talking to various German personnel in Paris about his idea for Abadan. But Germany's attack on the USSR was launched on June 22, 1941, and was the highest priority. Getting the decision-makers' attention for Abadan wasn't easy. Dr. Nikolas Bensmann, the Abwehr oil specialist, was believed to be in Paris at this time and may have heard of the scheme.[151] Bedaux was in contact with Julius Westrick, who was on the German embassy staff. The two had first met in 1935. Bedaux's offices in Paris were at 53 Avenue Hoche, in the same building, described as a former mansion, as a purchasing agency that was a cover for the operations of Andreas Folmer, an Abwehr officer.[152]

---

[149]   Paul Leverkühn, *German Military Intelligence,* 8.

[150]   Ibid., 9.

[151]   Bensmann would have been the ideal Abwehr agent handler for Bedaux. Having spent some years in the United States, he spoke English fluently with an American accent.

[152]   Christer Jorgensen, *Hitler's Espionage Machine,* 179.

What we definitely know is that Julius Westrick invited Bedaux to Berlin in October-November 1941, where he was debriefed by Abwehr personnel.[153] At first the Abadan idea was "condemned as fantastic."[154] But after the Speer ministry and Abteilung II of the Abwehr—headed by Colonel Erwin von Lahousen—evaluated it, the scheme was found to be feasible. Von Lahousen's department, Abteilung II, was responsible for sabotage and special operations.[155] Karl Strodil, the department's sabotage expert, had been assigned to review the plan, and he approved it.[156] Although the British and their new Russian ally had in August 1941 occupied the north and southern regions of Iran, Germany had plenty of resources on the ground to assist in an attack on Abadan. There were several thousand Germans in Iran, many in key positions in the country's communications and transportation system.

General Rommel's army in North Africa was still a threat to Egypt and the Suez Canal. Germany's armies in the USSR were threatening the Caucasus. The Brandenburg German Special Forces was deployed undercover throughout the region and attached to Colonel von Lahousen's Abteilung II

---

[153] Bedaux met with Abwehr oil specialist Nikolas Bensmann, who introduced him to Professor Edrou. (Nigel West, *Guy Liddell Diaries, Vol. II*, 143.)

[154] Paul Leverkühn, *German Military Intelligence*, 9.

[155] Von Lahousen, a professional Austrian Army officer prior to the annexation of Austria, had been responsible for the collection and evaluation of intelligence on Czechoslovakia and Poland. Recruited by Canaris, he was promoted rapidly and in 1943 was a major general when he was transferred to the Russian front. Von Lahousen, an avowed anti-Nazi, was the first prosecution witness at the Nuremberg Trials.

[156] Christer Jorgensen, *Hitler's Espionage Machine*, 179.

of the Abwehr. Organized in Poland from a special operations unit, the Special Forces evolved into a division strength organization, trained in sabotage and special operations. Members had to speak at least one foreign language.

There was an Arab combat unit called a German-Arabic Training Division based in Greece under the command of a Luftwaffe general, Hellmuth Felmy (1885-1965). Felmy was selected for the mission because of his Middle East experience in the First World War. His mission was to support the putsch attempt, or coup d'état, of Raschid Ali al-Gailani in Baghdad. The unit was to advance into Baghdad and Basra as part of a German Orient Corps after the Caucasus was conquered.[157] The attack on the USSR on June 22, 1941, was launched with 152 divisions, 3580 tanks, 2740 aircraft, and 3 million men. The immediate target was Moscow before winter arrived.[158]

Another early objective was the Caucasus, leading to the important oil fields. To support this effort called Operation Shamyl, a revolt of the local population was planned.[159]

A strong advocate for exploiting the Middle East was the German ambassador and Vice Chancellor under the Führer, Franz von Papen. Hitler, believing that Moscow could be captured quickly in the early months of his advance, approved a plan for German expansion in the Middle East. Germany planned a greater Arab Union that would be dependent on Germany and Italy.[160]

---

[157] Wolfgang Schwanitz, *Germany and the Middle East*, 203.

[158] Heinz Höhne, *Canaris*, 460.

[159] Shamyl (1797-1871) was a legendary leader of the Caucasus tribes in their wars against the Russians. (Ibid., 491.)

[160] Wolfgang Schwanitz, *Germany and the Middle East*, 95.

Bedaux negotiated as well as discussed while in Berlin. Von Lahousen's diary entry dated December 31, 1941,[161] indicated that Bedaux wanted the German rank of lieutenant general in the Wehrmacht, and also to become a German citizen.[162] The Abadan project was put on hold because the German advance in the USSR had come to a halt in the bitter winter of 1941, and it never again came up for consideration. Contact with Bedaux, however, continued.

There were a number of reasons why the Bedaux project wasn't launched. It had been under discussion for some time. The Arabists in the various German services would have favored it as a part of a master plan to gain control of the Middle East and its oil. This also may potentially have led to the weakening of Britain's hold on India, the jewel of the empire. But the Middle East was not a priority for Adolf Hitler. He envisaged a world dominated by Germany, and in which Britain could keep its empire, but in a subservient role. His principal aims were to achieve Lebensraum in Eastern Europe, rid the world of Bolshevism, and create a master race—and leave North Africa and the Middle East to the Italian allies.

The Italians failed, however, and Hitler's attention was focused on the war in the East. He and the General Staff

---

[161] Von Lahousen met with the Grand Mufti of Jerusalem on December 11, 1941, in Berlin on the day Germany declared war on the United States. (Paul Leverkühn, *German Military Intelligence*, 41.)

[162] Sources include General Lahousen's *Tagebuch*, or diary (RW 5/V 498, p. 180-181); and *Institut für Zeitgeschichte* in Munich archive.

believed that a Blitzkrieg of eight to twelve weeks would bring them to Moscow, but it stalled.[163]

Had the campaign in the Caucasus moved forward, Charles Bedaux may have become a general officer in the Wehrmacht and joined his friend, Franz Albrecht Medicus, in a prisoner-of-war compound. The Axis powers were doomed to lose the war once the United States entered the conflict.

Fritz Grobba,[164] one of Germany's most knowledgeable and experienced diplomats on the Middle East, wrote in a 1957 report that the Reich failed to exploit the opportunities in Caucasus during the Second World War due to the anti-Hitler opposition of men such as Admiral Canaris.[165]

---

[163] On July 14, 1941, in a meeting with the Japanese ambassador, Hitler proposed that after the victory in Russia, the two allies jointly attack the United States. (Klaus Hildebrand, *The Foreign Policy*, 113.)

[164] Grobba served in the Middle East at various times between 1913 and 1941. He was in Baghdad when Rashid al-Gailani gained control in April 1941. Grobba died in 1973.

[165] Wolfgang Schwanitz, *Germany and the Middle East*, 110.)

AFRICA

Not long after the occupation of France, Charles Bedaux began to play a role in the economics and politics of the new situation. His know-how and experience were of immediate interest to both Vichy and the German authorities in Paris. On the German side, he knew Otto Abetz, the German ambassador in Paris. He was a friend of Georg von Stauss, a director of Germany's largest bank and vice president of the Reichstag, and we know that Germany's intelligence service was very much aware of Charles Bedaux. Bedaux's travels had given him an overview of various areas that few others possessed. The French saw him as someone who could improve the productivity of various enterprises. The German government saw him as an entrepreneur and a very useful source.

There were two major political goals of the Vichy government under Pétain-Laval and Admiral Darlan, who had taken over from Laval in December 1940: to demonstrate that France could be a useful partner to the Third Reich, and to keep control of the overseas colonial empire. Exports from the African interests were critical to maintain France's standard of living.

After the First World War, France considered the British their only competition in Africa. Germany was pretty much out of the picture, having started late in claiming its colonies in East Africa (Tanzania, Togoland, and Cameroon) during the late nineteenth and early twentieth centuries, and having lost it all after the First World War.

It would be more accurate to say it was no longer official German government policy to pursue territory in Africa under the Weimar Republic or even under Hitler. But Hitler pretended to have an interest in Africa as a tactical negotiating chip when dealing with the British during the run-up to the Second World War. He thought the future for the Reich was absolute control of the European continent, and wanted Lebensraum for the Aryan race, which would eventually dominate the world. There were others in the German government and military, however, who were more favorably deposed and kept an open mind to Africa's possibilities.

One of the strongest advocates for colonies was a banker, Kurt Weigelt, a director of Deutsche Bank and an associate of Georg von Stauss's. Weigelt had been involved with the colonial economy since before the First World War. He owned a banana plantation in the British Cameroons. He had joined the SS in 1934 and the Nazi Party in 1937, and was designated to play a key role in a ministry for colonial affairs, should such a ministry be established. There was, in fact, a "shadow colonial minister" with an office in the Ribbentrop Ministry of Foreign Affairs: Franz Xaver Ritter von Epp, an early Hitler follower. His views about the value of colonies were shared by Hjalmar Schacht and Erhard

Milch, who was then state secretary in Hermann Göring's Air Ministry.[166]

In the early years of the Third Reich, Weigelt proposed the formation of a Franco-German company to increase German trade with France's overseas empire.[167] But even among Hitler's closest associates, there was a lack of clarity about the Führer's real position. A view he expressed on August 25, 1939, just days before the attack on Poland, in a conversation with the British ambassador Sir Neville Henderson was this: Allow the British to keep their empire, but give him a free hand on the Continent and make some minor corrections in the colonial distribution of Africa.[168]

Within the German military, it was Admiral Eric Räder, the commander of Germany's naval forces, who in a memorandum to Hitler on June 3, 1940, envisioned the Reich's colonial empire to stretch across central Africa from the Atlantic coast to the Indian Ocean.

From the beginning, a Vichy objective was to get the Third Reich to accept France as a junior partner in the New Europe by becoming a colonial and maritime link to an African reserve of critical resources. Vichy perceived the African colonies as compensation for its losses in Europe, and their development dated back to the glorious time of Napoleon.

But there were others interested in Africa. Italy's leader, Mussolini, conquered Ethiopia in the 1930s, and had ambitions to expand his empire at the cost of the British.

---

[166] Milch, who was reputed to be half-Jewish, had the wartime rank of Field Marshal in the *Luftwaffe*.

[167] Lothar Gall, *The Deutsche Bank*, 320.

[168] In 1938 the British prime minister Neville Chamberlain had proposed in cabinet discussions that Germany be given certain African colonies to administer.

For Great Britain, Africa meant the Suez Canal, the lifeline to the East. Amid these crosscurrents, Charles Bedaux was to play an important role, but one that led to his eventual downfall.

In July 1940, even before a Vichy government was in place, the Germans discovered on the desk of General Charles Huntzinger, the French representative to the Armistice Commission at Wiesbaden, a memorandum proposing that the French army in the Middle East seize control of the Iraqi oil fields of Mosul and Kirkuk for the "account of France, Germany and Italy." The three countries would then become stockholders of the Iraqi Petroleum Company and remove it from the control of the "Anglo-Saxon Trusts."[169]

The intent obviously was for the document to be found, and in many ways it reflected the hopes and aspirations of many of the political and military leaders of a defeated France. Without a doubt, it influenced the thinking of Otto Abetz, and possibly some of the members of the Abwehr. France had troops in Syria as well as North Africa. Iraq, a British protectorate, had experienced several putsch attempts from 1925 to 1940. Germany was interested in the oil fields of the Middle East, and at about this time Charles Bedaux was making known to various Germans his ideas on the subject.

On August 28, 1940, Pierre Laval—in a conversation with Friedrich Grimm, the renowned German lawyer now on the Abetz embassy staff—suggested that France could be

---

[169] Robert Paxton, *Vichy France*, 59.

compensated with parts of British Africa for losing Alsace to Germany.[170] [171]

In the meantime, General Charles de Gaulle, who had reached London after France's defeat and became the leader of the Free French Forces through a bloodless coup in August 1940, gained control of French Equatorial Africa. With the help of the British, he threatened French West Africa.

On October 24, 1940, Hitler met with Pétain at Montoire. The French hero of the First World War Battle of Verdun agreed to collaborate with the Germans. In return, he would be recognized by the New Europe and compensated with colonial territory taken from the British.[172]

In a meeting with the Soviet foreign minister Molotov on November 12, 1940, von Ribbentrop even suggested that Germany would next expand Lebensraum through Central Africa, an obvious attempt to throw off the wily Russian from Germany's real goal to conquer eastward.[173]

When the war began, German lacked the key resources needed to supply its armaments industry. It had stockpiled critical materials—oil, copper, aluminum—but Hitler, being ever the gambler, believed that a Blitzkrieg strategy would soon bring re-supply. It did. But now the questions were these: How to improve productivity of the new conquests? How to best exploit the opportunities of French

---

[170] Ibid., 65.

[171] In a meeting between Grimm and Laval on March 8, 1942, the French politician continued to stress the opportunities for a joint Franco-German effort for harvesting Africa's wealth and helping Europe to be independent of overseas suppliers. (BAKoblenz, N 1120/5, 49.)

[172] William Shirer, *The Rise and Fall of the Third Reich*, 815.

[173] Ibid., 804.

Africa? How to get the oil out of the Middle East? These questions became new playing fields for Charles Bedaux as if all of his previous experience had trained the man for the role he was about to perform.

Bedaux had already served the French Government in an advisory role on at least two occasions. The first was in 1936, soon after the Léon Blum's Popular Front came to power, when he participated in the Matignon meeting in which the settlement of the strikes that had shut down most of France's economy was negotiated. The second was on assignment from the Ministry of Armaments at the start of the war. We have already discussed both of these in some detail. The question of improving productivity by increasing the output of the Kenadsa coal mines in Morocco also concerned the Vichy Government in 1940-41, just as it had in 1939. Once again, the French-American consultant was called upon to help.

Before leaving for Africa, Bedaux met with Otto Abetz, the German ambassador in Paris, who had recently been informed of the dismissal of Pierre Laval by Marshal Pétain. Bedaux was asked by Abetz to discuss with General Maxime Weygand, delegate general to French colonial Africa, whether he would be interested in joining the Vichy Government. Bedaux approached Weygand and, as expected, Weygand refused. How could anyone but a trusted German agent be given such a mission? Charles Bedaux was given this assignment only one year before Germany declared war on the United States.

Bedaux's Kenadsa coal project, a follow-up to his earlier French Third Republic consultancy, moved forward with the support of the German occupiers. A hundred miles of railway was constructed between Colomb-Béchar and Ben-Abes on the Oran main line. The workers were

Berber, African, POWs from Poland and Czechoslovakia, and Spanish internees from Spain's Civil War, all under the direction of German engineers. Germany was ready to support the Kenadsa effort because of its fear of a severe coal shortage in Occupied France as reported in a study dated September 1940.[174] An estimated two hundred thousand dollars in scarce equipment was released by the occupation administration for the project. There was even some discussion about the feasibility of having Krupp and Mannesmann, two major German armament manufactures, build plants in the Kenadsa area.

In March 1941, Norman Fleming of Planning Associated Industrial Consultants of London, the successor company to the Bedaux consultancy, informed the British Trading with the Enemy branch that Bedaux was reorganizing the French coal industry. The information came in a letter to Colwell Carney, the former Bedaux manager, in the United States.[175] Carney was one of the first American engineers hired by Bedaux in the 1920s, and had been one of the managers of the London office. With this information, British intelligence was alerted to the activities of the man who hosted the wedding of the Duke and Duchess of Windsor. One would have guessed that this news would have served as a warning signal in the Allied offices.

In 1941, on one of Bedaux's visits to Vichy, he met again with Marshal Pétain. Bedaux had first met Pétain in 1926 in a chance encounter at the Invalides in Paris. At that time, Bedaux had promised the hero of Verdun that he would one

---

[174] MAFreiburg, RW 303, p. 6-8.
[175] Peter Allen, *The Crown and the Swastika*, 157.

day build a monument on that famous battleground of the First World War to commemorate the great victory.[176]

Bedaux took this opportunity to lecture Pétain about his favorite economic idea, "equivalism." For years, Bedaux had believed that he could cure the world's economic ills with various theories that he'd developed. For example, in an August 1939 meeting with Hjalmar Schacht, the Reichsbank president, Bedaux suggested that the unit of human energy, which he named "B," could replace the gold standard to support a nation's currency. Schacht dismissed the idea out of hand, embarrassing Georg von Stauss, who had arranged the dinner.

Equivalism was an idea that Bedaux had been developing since the early days in Grand Rapids, where he launched his consultancy in 1915. Equivalism was intended to build an ideal world in which labor, management, and the community would live together in harmony. Money would no longer be required, and in its place would be the Bedaux Bs. Equivalism would replace capitalism and communism.

Bedaux had explained his idea to Pétain in great detail, but Pétain had probably understood very little. After all, it was Pétain who in 1940 had said that Vichy France "will become what it should have never ceased being, an essentially agricultural nation."[177] This fundamental, basic belief was strongly ingrained in the mind of the Vichy leader, who saw himself as France's savior. He accepted the idea of the fast-talking, smooth salesman Charles Bedaux,

---

[176] The monument was to be based on the model of Francois Cogné's sculpture of Pétain on horseback. Pétain kept this figure in his office in Vichy.

[177] Herbert Lottman, *Pétain: Hero or Traitor?* 264.

however, and agreed to test-market the French-American's dream of equivalism.

The town of Roquefort—located 68 miles (110 km) northeast of Bayonne, with a population of 1200—was selected for the test. Bedaux assigned a team of engineers to work on the project from March to December 1941. The forests in the Roquefort area were rich in briar roots, for which Bedaux saw the potential to convert to gasogenes to power automobiles. The Germans looked in on the Roquefort project from time to time, but concluded that it wasn't a practical way to solve France's ills. But to Bedaux, the goal of equivalism was to eliminate "the parasites collecting unearned income."[178]

Bedaux's next project—and what would be his last project for either Vichy France or the Third Reich—was to do what no one else had been able to accomplish: to conquer the Sahara Desert.

For many decades, different governments and business interests had dreamed of developing a transportation system to link the Saharan colonies and dependencies. But there were many obstacles to overcome, and first and foremost was the terrain, the desert. Where would the water come from to support the labor? The many naysayers and the bureaucrats found it difficult to cooperate. It would take a big idea, a looming shortage on the mainland (the mother country), and a dictatorship to change the rules on the playing field.

The German occupiers and the French collaborators had to find a new source of nutrition to allay the serious

---

[178] Jim Christy, *The Price of Power*, 315.

food shortages now plaguing the continent.[179] French farms suffered from a labor shortage since 36 percent of the French prisoners of war were agricultural workers. Large quantities of French foodstuffs were requisitioned by the Germans and sent to Germany.[180] Edible oil, rich in nutrients, could help alleviate the problem.

Bedaux was very qualified to discuss Africa's economy and how best to exploit its resources. Since the late 1920s he had offices in South Africa and clients that included two-thirds of the gold fields of Rhodesia, the diamond mines of South Africa, and the copper mines of the Belgian Congo.

His five-month, 9500-mile expedition in 1929—starting in Kenya, and ending in Morocco—was the first of Bedaux's several African treks in the pre-war years, and was probably when his dreams of exploiting the vast undeveloped areas of Africa began to evolve.

To solve the problem of shortages of critical nutrients in Europe, Bedaux envisaged the possibility of making the Sahara bloom.

We know that Bedaux was in frequent contact with Georg von Stauss of Deutsche Bank. Kurt Weigelt, a bank director and strong advocate of German investment in Africa, had in the pre-war years proposed the creation of a Franco-German company to increase German trade with France's African colonies.[181] It was an idea that never

---

[179] The Germans even considered developing peanut plantations in the newly conquered Ukraine to produce edible oil. The adult French citizen was estimated to have a daily diet of 1500 calories, less than that of the people of Romania, Bulgaria, and Hungary.

[180] Robert Paxton, *Vichy France*, 360.

[181] Lothar Gall, *The Deutsche Bank*, 320.

gained the support of the Nazi government, but never lost the interest of German industrial-financial circles. In November 1941, while in Berlin on Abwehr business, Bedaux spent a long weekend at Burg Schlitz, von Stauss's estate in Mecklenburg. We can assume that business matters were on the agenda. It is likely that Bedaux, having recently returned from Africa, would have discussed the possibility of setting up a company to exploit the development of trade with the French territories.[182]

Could von Stauss have been interested in investing in such an enterprise? Would Deutsche Bank potentially be involved? Von Stauss as an individual would have been a possibility, but the bank wouldn't have qualified as easily. The Nazi government wasn't in favor of German-French joint companies, but if this hadn't been the case, von Stauss probably would have brought the bank into the deal. After all, Deutsche Bank had always been active internationally.[183] Von Stauss, for whom Bedaux had the greatest respect, was described as a "master of intrigues involving the (Nazi) party,"[184] and would have been an ideal candidate for such a discussion.

The Bedaux plan to conquer the Saharan Desert and exploit its agricultural wealth would take roughly four years to complete. The pipeline to be built had a triple function. It was to start in an oasis in Algeria between Fez and Colomb-Béchar and "continue south across the Sahara for two thousand miles, between the Grand Erg and Igrid sand dunes, through the valleys of the Atlas Mountains, and

---

[182] Deutsche Bank archives don't have any evidence of von Stauss correspondence on the subject.

[183] Ibid., 318.

[184] Ibid., 345.

across the Sudan to the port town of Gao on the Niger River, the last unused fertile spot of Africa."[185] The pipeline would carry water south from the oasis to provide for the laborers building it, and to make it possible for a railroad to be constructed across the Sahara parallel to the pipeline. When the pipeline reached Gao, it was then to transport peanut oil from the Niger to the north to help alleviate the nutrition problem in Europe.

The seven-inch pipeline would require 60,000 tons of steel, which had to be released by the Nazi government. It would take an estimated nine months to build from the Algerian oasis to the Niger River. While the construction was going on, peanut plantations would be expanded along the Niger River and small presses would be positioned to produce peanut oil. By 1946 at the latest, the pipeline would no longer be used for water, and instead it would ship 250,000 tons of peanut oil a year. The railroad, which would reach Gao in 1946, would by 1944 have arrived at the Quallen oasis. By then, an additional pipeline from the Niger River to Quallen would be ready to refresh the laborers the rest of the way. When this pipeline was no longer needed for railroad construction, it would be used to "water the desert and make it bloom." There were also two more peanut oil pipelines, a gasoline pipeline, and a highway for trucks planned.

The railroad was to be 1400 miles long and cost the French $30 million, about what they paid the German occupation every two weeks. The railroad would branch west through Timbuktu to the river town of Bamako, the inland terminal of the French railroad to Dakar, on the Atlantic Ocean. That link would allow troop train transports

---

[185]   Janet Flanner, "Annals of Collaboration," *The New Yorker*.

from the Mediterranean city of Oran, Algeria, to get to a jumping-off point at Dakar, Senegal, on the Atlantic. After the conquest of Europe, German military planners would have the option of launching a paratroop invasion of South America.[186] The railroad received widespread publicity in the Nazi press, but the peanut oil pipeline was still the priority. The pipeline was the zenith moment of Bedaux's collaboration, and almost entirely overt. And it wouldn't have been conceivable without the intervention and approval of Bedaux's Abwehr handlers.

---

[186] Flights from the United States to West Africa flew via Brazil, the route taken from Africa when Bedaux was returned to Miami after his capture.

PEANUTS, THE POTENTIAL SOLUTION

In the meantime, the war continued to expand. The Japanese attacked the United States at Pearl Harbor on December 7, 1941, and Hitler, in his wisdom, ordered a declaration of war on December 11 in support of his Asian ally. This immediately turned Charles and Fern Bedaux into enemy aliens, and the well-known German efficiency wasn't at its best because the Abwehr collaborator and his wife were interned for several weeks.[187]

In March 1942, a group of French businessmen met in Paris to discuss the launching of a company to study the increase of agricultural exports from French Africa. Attending the meeting were personnel from Bedaux's company in France; Jean Goy, CEO of the *Société Samoa* and chairman of the UNC, the French veterans' organization,

---

[187] While he was interned, there was serious discussion at the top level of the Abwehr organization about Bedaux's use in the so-called Abadan project.

and a member of the French Parliament in the 1930s[188]; Francis Peyrissac, CEO of Peyrissac and Cie. in Bordeaux, and owner of various enterprises in French West Africa; M. Annet, a university lecturer and specialist in colonial agricultural; and RR 2615 "Charles."

The writer of the report from which I base my commentary[189] was an Abwehr officer from "Nest Bremen," and was brought into the meeting and introduced as a specialist by RR 2615 "Charles." ("Charles" was probably Charles Bedaux, who had been identified as Abwehr source RR 2615.[190])

Nikolas Bensmann, the German patent lawyer for the Texas Oil Company, was known to be in Paris at the time, probably on assignment for Bedaux's handling and debriefing. Considered the Abwehr's leading oil specialist, Bensmann produced more first-rate intelligence than any other member of the Bremen sub-branch to which he was assigned.[191] The report described the meeting's discussions, including the attitudes and views of leading personalities in the colonial administration. Source RR 2615 was the participant who questioned Peyrissac in detail about the political aims of Governor-General Boisson of West

---

[188]   Goy first met Hitler in 1934. On February 23, 1941, at a mass meeting that he co-chaired at the Salle Wagram, which was called to get France to collaborate with Germany.

[189]   MAFreiburg W VI/252.

[190]   The reporter from Nest Bremen, a key Abwehr post specializing in the handling of American sources, was probably Nikolas Bensmann.

[191]   Ladislas Farrago, *Game of the Foxes*, 405.

Africa.[192] Boisson, with an army of four hundred thousand men at his disposal, would have to cooperate. If he refused, Vichy wouldn't have the resources for counteraction. Vichy would have to agree to support the economic development of West Africa and be a supplier for Europe, for which there had not been much enthusiasm in the past.

Goy said that Europe had to be defended against not only communism but also the economic competition from Japan and the United States. But Boisson was reluctant to support development because he feared that West Africa would become a target for invasion by the Anglo-Saxons. He would agree to support the development effort only if he was convinced that Vichy would defend West Africa against the British and Americans. Vichy, in turn, had to understand that the development of West Africa would be to the economic advantage of France regardless of the war's outcome. After discussion, the participants agreed to organize a company by March 30, 1942, with startup capital of FF 1 million (one million French francs) to study West Africa investment possibilities.

The investors were RR 2615 "Charles," Goy, Peyrissac, and the Marquis de Laborde, the brother of Admiral de Laborde, the commander of the French Mediterranean naval fleet. A conference about increasing the production of peanuts in French Africa had preceded the meeting on the company formation. The report was prepared by "Abwehr Wi,"—a designation indicating that the secret intelligence service Abwehr I (i.e., active espionage) was directly

---

[192] Pierre Francois Boisson, 1894-1948, had resisted General de Gaulle's Free French invasion of Dakar. He later switched loyalties to de Gaulle.

involved, and "Wi" economic and commercial information was the subject.[193]

The conference concluded that peanut oil production would have to be increased ten-fold to meet the needs of continental Europe. The good that this would bring about included:

- French economic improvements
- Continued operation of France's industries with vegetable (peanut) oil as a "lubricant"
- Strengthening the "new Europe"

But this was only achievable if control of the French colonial empire was retained.

The report with RR 2615 "Charles" as a participant is certainly proof positive that the Abwehr gave Charles Bedaux a source identity number, making him an engaged collaborator with an American enemy during wartime.

If the Vichy government did not cooperate in the development of the colonies, the *Friedensregelung*, or armistice, would be in jeopardy. Also, the French colonies' native populations would be vulnerable to propaganda emanating from the neighboring British colonies. But the longer-term danger was that the native populations would turn against their white rulers. Mistreatment of Muslims in the colonies had already led to tensions.

Hitler's New Order was possible only if the people's basic nutritional needs were met. If a solution couldn't be found, worker productivity would fall and the war economy would be disrupted. For various reasons, the French colonial administration had done very little to encourage

---

[193] The report on the short conference that preceded the meeting is an attachment in MAFreiburg WI VI/2527.

economic development. For one, the leadership believed that if colonies became productive, this would compete with French agriculture and result in an oversupply and a fall in price.[194] Many French leaders believed that keeping French farmers happy was critical to the nation's wellbeing. Things have not changed that much today.

The German view was that Europe could be competitive against and independent of America and Asia only if Africa was developed and integrated into Europe's economy. The stakes were enormous. If France, that is Vichy, ignored the possibilities, the French-German armistice would have been endangered and France may have lost its African empire.

The new company had its bylaws notarized on March 30, 1942. Fernand de Brinon, the Vichy ambassador to the German occupation administration in Paris, was told to ensure the cooperation of the Vichy government on the project.[195] The company's name was "*Syndicat d'Études du Continent Africain pour le Transport des Huiles Africaines,*" and Banque de Paris et des Pay-Bas was to issue the bonds to finance the project. On September 15, 1942, thirty-year bonds for FF 350 million paying 3.5 percent interest guaranteed by the French government came on the market to finance the construction of the Trans-Saharan Railway, and more financing would follow.[196]

Leading banks would sell the bonds. These banks would certainly have included Worms Bank, whose executives held key positions in Pétain's Vichy government; and Stein Bank

---

[194] Indochina had already fallen to the Japanese.

[195] DeBrinon, a former journalist who interviewed Hitler in the 1930s and a friend of Laval's, encouraged the skeptical premier to support the project. DeBrinon was tried and executed in 1947 for collaborating with the Reich.

[196] Pressedienst Hansa, Oct. 1, 1942.

of Cologne, headed by Kurt von Schröder, a leading figure in German banking circles. In the 1920s, von Schröder was a member of *Deutsche Volkspartei* (DVP), the German People's Party, along with Georg von Stauss.[197] With Hitler's coming to power, von Schröder joined the Nazi Party and became a founder of Heinrich Himmler's Circle of Friends, which lent financial support to the leader of the S.S. Von Schröder was also a board member of ITT's German companies, of which Gerhard Westrick was chairman.[198]

Various authors have claimed that the company's name was Trans-Africa Company and that Deutsche Bank was involved. A search of the bank archives, however, shows no evidence to support this. The bank was certainly interested in development in France—as indicated in correspondence dated February 26, 1941, from Hauptmann Mertens, Feldpostnr. 00666 1, to Hermann Abs (the Deutsche Bank director responsible for international business) concerning the assignment of Barnaud of Worms Bank to the Vichy cabinet responsible for German-French cooperation.[199]

---

[197] It was at von Schröder's home on Jan. 4, 1933, where Franz von Papen met with Hitler and an agreement was made that brought the Nazis to power.

[198] At the end of the war, von Schröder was found in a holding camp for SS members, wearing a uniform of a simple SS soldier. He was tried by a German court in 1947 and sentenced to three month's imprisonment and the payment of a nominal fine. Released on June 11, 1948, he retired to his estate, Hohenstein, where he lived until his death on November 4, 1966.

[199] Worms Bank and Deutsche Bank were destined to have a closer relationship, and this will be discussed in a later chapter.

The seven-inch pipeline required the release of sixty thousand tons of steel from Europe's mills. This was no small enterprise, and the Abwehr gave it very high priority. In accordance with Abwehr leader Admiral Canaris's decentralization policy, the Abwehr in France had authority to promote the peanut oil venture without much intervention from headquarters.

The harvested peanuts would have had to be processed with small presses or mincing machines scattered throughout France and Germany. These machines were to be shipped to Africa for that purpose. The end product, 250,000 tons of peanut (vegetable) oil to be shipped annually from Africa to Europe, was an impressive figure when compared to the output of France's major pre-war supplier of peanut oil, Lesieur. Founded in 1908, Lesieur had large peanut plantations in French West Africa and it shipped the peanuts to a plant in Dunkirk, France, to be processed into oil. In 1938, the plant processed 120,000 tons of peanuts. From this came 45,000 tons of crude peanut oil, 40,000 tons of refined (edible) peanut oil, 55,000 tons of oil cakes, and 11,000 tons of soap.[200]

The president of Lesieur was Jacques Lemaigre Dubreuil, who was born in 1894. He served in the First World War, and in the mid 1920s married a daughter of the company's founder. In the 1930s he became a leader of the Taxpayer League, an organization dedicated to fighting government waste and corruption. In 1935 he became the group's president, and after visiting Hitler he's quoted as having said: "A great people is beginning anew under the

---

[200] William H. Hoisington, Jr., *A Businessman in Politics*, 188.

direction of a leader, who knows what he wants, and who vigorously applies his principles."[201]

The pre-war years in France were noteworthy for labor-management strife, general strikes, the 1934 putsch attempt, the Popular Front, and fear of communism's spread. The right reacted by creating pro-fascist newspapers and organizations, often funded by leading industrialists.

One of the most violent groups was La Cagoule, "the hooded ones," which was ready to turn to assassination to achieve its objectives. Some authors have claimed that Lemaigre Dubreuil was a member.[202] As Professor Hoisington in his work on this very interesting character points out, "Lemaigre was difficult to get along with. He said what he thought, rarely softening his bluntness or hiding his feelings . . . such a man had few really close friends."[203]

Lemaigre participated in a committee formed in March 1940 to study the possibility of building factories in Senegal to process the peanut crop, an idea that had originated with Georges Mandel,[204] the pre-war colonial minister.[205] But

---

[201]   Ibid., 50.

[202]   In the post war years, he successfully sued to clear his name. (Ibid.)

[203]   Ibid.

[204]   Georges Mandel (1885-1944): Journalist, politician, and resistance leader. He was minister of overseas France and her colonies from 1938 until May 18, 1940. After the German invasion, he escaped to French North Africa. On Laval's orders he was brought back to France as a prisoner and turned over to the Gestapo in November 1942. On July 7, 1944, the *Milice*, the French collaborationist police, executed Mandell.

[205]   Ibid., 190.

time ran out before it could be implemented. France was hit with the German Blitzkrieg, and by the second half of June 1940, the battle for France was over.

In the early days of the Vichy government, October 1940, Félix Adolphe Eboué, governor-general of French equatorial Africa and "an enthusiast" of African industrialization, put forward a plan for expanding peanut processing in West Africa. But there was not much enthusiasm from French business circles to invest or to otherwise support this idea.[206] Lemaigre Dubreuil was often in Africa, and in a January 2, 1941, letter to the Vichy government on behalf of the Lesieur company, he agreed to construct and operate peanut processing factories in Senegal and North Africa. The Vichy government quickly approved his proposal, and with the consent of the German occupation administration, entire sections of the Dunkirk factory were shipped to Africa.

Did Lemaigre have a role in the peanut oil pipeline scheme? Did the two men, Charles Bedaux and Jacques Lemaigre Dubreuil, cooperate in any way? Both certainly had an interest in developing the same area of French Africa; their paths must have crossed. Bedaux, through his various contacts, would have heard of Lemaigre's plan to shift production of peanut oil from Dunkirk to Africa—he had been engaged by Vichy and had the occupation administration's support to solve some of the transportation bottleneck problems in North Africa. Bedaux's pipeline scheme was a logical follow-up. Lemaigre must have been aware of the pipeline project; it was in the press.[207] Lemaigre

---

[206]   Ibid., 191.

[207]   Prof. Hoisington, with whom I had contact, spent many years researching Lemaigre, but never found that the two had contact with one another.

was also one of the conspirators in North Africa who assisted Robert Murphy, the American diplomat, in preparing the way for the Allied landings in November 1942.[208]

Well, let's first take a look at the Bedaux plan to encourage the economic development of French Africa. There were three functions to the project that was to start in an Algerian oasis somewhere between the Fez River and Colomb-Bechar. A seven-inch steel pipeline was to extend two thousand miles to the south, crossing the Sahara between Grand Erg and the Igisti sand dunes. The pipeline at first would carry water for the construction crew that was to build a railroad to the south.

On its completion in an estimated nine months, the pipeline was to be used to transport peanut oil from the plantations along the Niger River. The peanut plantations were to be expanded ten-fold, contributing significantly to Europe's nutrition requirements. The pipeline, the first of three in the plan, would transport 250,000 tons of peanut oil per annum. In addition, a gasoline pipeline and a highway for truck transport were to be built. The railroad would have a branch from Timbuktu to the river town of Bamako, where it would connect with the line to Dakar. This linkup would allow troop transports from Oran to Dakar and give the German high command an option to launch a paratroop assault against South American targets. Completion date was to be 1946.

---

[208] In July 1944, Lemaigre tried to organize contact between Laval and Washington, D.C., in an attempt to bring about a compromise peace between the Allies and the Reich in order to stop the advancing Soviet forces. Von Ribbentrop, however, ordered an immediate halt to German participation. (Robert Paxton, *Vichy France*, 328.)

The pipeline project wasn't a secret. On the contrary, it received wide press coverage from Vichy to Berlin, including a photo of Bedaux. To get moving, Bedaux received special passes issued by Otto Abetz on behalf of the German occupation administration and Pierre Laval, the Vichy premier. Laval, always the practical politician, thought the idea of building a railroad crossing the Sahara slightly insane, but he reluctantly issued the pass. Both passes ordered German and French officials to cooperate and gave the project the highest priority.

During the summer of 1942, the Swiss ambassador, acting on behalf of the United States government, advised Charles and Fern Bedaux to return to the United States. They refused. Bedaux claimed he was on a humanitarian mission to repair the ills of war, and would not cease his efforts. On September 24, 1942, in a typical German bureaucratic lapse, Bedaux was picked up in Paris in a Gestapo sweep, but was released after a few days when the Abwehr intervened.

Having had invested in the survey company, was there a profit motive in Bedaux's plans to conquer the Sahara Desert? Although the pipelines and the railroad were to become the property of the French government, the peanut plantations and peanut oil would have given investors a significant return. Money never really drove Bedaux; he just assumed it would be there by virtue of his accomplishments. The motivation that drove Bedaux was to do what had never been done before: to conquer the Sahara.

To finance the various construction projects beyond the Trans-Saharan Railway, a bond issue was planned but never implemented. Banque Paribas was to coordinate the financial side, with input from Worms Bank and Stein Bank in Cologne, headed by Kurt von Schröder. From the Abwehr perspective, key personalities in the Vichy government and collaborators in French industry were eager to do their part in demonstrating their loyalty to the New Order—and for the financial rewards the desert project would bring.

On a visit to Vichy on July 22, 1942, Bedaux met with Pickney Tuck, the U.S. *chargé d'affaires*, and described the project in detail. After the meeting, in a report to Washington, Tuck said of Bedaux: "I believe this astonishing person can be classified as mentally immoral. He apparently lacks the tradition and background which should make him realize that there is anything wrong, as an American citizen, in his open association with our declared enemies . . . he may be attempting to find for himself a safe place in the New Order."[209]

The project would have required approval by the top echelons of the Third Reich, and would also have had an Abwehr military dimension. In his memoir, Paul Leverkühn, a major operative of the Abwehr who was chief of German espionage in Turkey and the Middle East, described Bedaux's survey mission as being organized in three columns.[210] Officers of the French Colonial Service, with special expertise of the terrain, were attached to the project and equipped with special motor vehicles to cross the desert. Abwehr agents were among the expedition personnel who were to report by radio anything of military interest. The left-wing column was especially important because it "was marching to the east from the Niger knee and in the general direction of the Tibesti Massif (Tibesti Moutains)."

---

[209] Charles Higham, *Trading with the Enemy*, 184.
[210] Paul Leverkühn, *German Military Intelligence*, 128-9.

Bedaux finally arrived by plane in Algiers on October 27, 1942. The Allied forces invaded North Africa on November 8.[211]

If the peanut oil pipeline project were to advance beyond the survey mission—for which Bedaux and others were in North Africa in late October-early November 1942—it would have required major capital investments by Vichy, the Third Reich, and individual investors. We must bear in mind the enormity of the plan to have pipelines, railroad, and highway traverse Saharan terrain for up to two thousand miles, and for peanut plantations and processing to expand ten-fold at the southern end. Had it been achieved, Bedaux's name would have been recognized in history books as one of the major African developers.

The Germans would, of course, expect to be compensated for its expenditures, which included technical and control manpower, equipment, sixty thousand tons of steel, and more. Diverting this much steel, a key commodity in armaments production, would certainly have required approval at the highest level of the Reich's economic leadership. At the end of the day, France would have been left holding the bag, but it would have owned the infrastructure, enabling its African empire's economy

---

211 One of the earliest supporters of Hitler's rise to power and his confidante on raising money, Wilhelm Keppler, in some of his post-war comments available in BAKoblenz Nr. 537-2 Fol. 1, defends Hitler against the July 20, 1944, conspirators, whom he describes as traitors. In Nr. 537-5 Fol. 1, Keppler kept a newspaper clipping from October 1948 describing British plans to develop peanut plantations in East Africa. Keppler's assignment in the Third Reich was state secretary of the Foreign Ministry, responsible for the Four Year Plan. He would have been informed of the Bedaux project.

to expand. There also may have been financial gain for individual investors in peanut plantations and processing. Agricultural development would have benefited by the opening of the European market. Industrialism of one kind or another would have certainly followed in the wake of the new transportation infrastructure.

All of this, of course, assumed that the hostilities would end in the near future.

The mindset prevalent in pre-war France, both in the colonial administration and in the government, was a kind of mercantilism. The colonies were viewed as markets for the motherland to exploit; their development was discouraged so that they would remain net importers, not competition. The French attitude toward its African possessions in the twentieth century was not unlike the British view of its American colonies in the eighteenth century, which led to the Revolutionary War. There were others in the business and banking world, however, with a different viewpoint about what the colonies represented. Among this group were Jacques Lemaigre Dubreuil, the Lesieur company director, and the Worms Bank management group.

Worms Bank, a private bank, was founded in Paris in 1850 by the Worms family, whose origin was believed to be Frankfurt. The bank had been created to finance the business affairs of the so-called Worms Group, which was active in shipbuilding, maritime services, and the coal trade. It held shares in more than one hundred companies. Before the war, it had important trading links with Great Britain and, consequently, when hostilities ended, immediately came under suspicion by the occupation authorities. The Jewish member of the three-man directorate, Hippolyte Worms, was forced to resign his post.[212] German commissioner Ziegesar of Commerzbank was appointed to monitor the bank's activities. Commerzbank, Germany's third-largest bank, had been a pre-war correspondent of Worms Bank.

Ziegesar's description of Gabriel Le Roy Ladurie, the salaried manager of Worms Bank, concluded that he was a highly qualified professional who was eager to develop economic relations between France and Germany.[213] On January 20, 1941, the Worms management group dined with Otto Abetz, the Reich's ambassador in Paris, and shortly thereafter many of them joined Admiral Darlan's Vichy government.[214]

Jean-Francis Darlan's policy was to seek a revival of France through maritime and colonial resources.[215] The so-called Worms Group was made up of well-educated experts who came from the France's *Grandes Écoles*, the elite schools. The Worms Group saw its role as governing without the corruption and tensions of the politicians in France's pre-war parliamentary system. Among this group was Jacques Barnaud, one of the the three top directors of Worms Bank, who in the Darlan cabinet occupied the position of chief economic negotiator with the Third Reich. Others included Pierre Pucheu, minister for industrial production and later minister of the interior, and the

---

[212] Hippolyte Worms, born in 1889 to a Catholic mother and Jewish father, was the grandson of the bank's founder.

[213] Worms Bank gave Commerzbank office space and assistance in starting up a French operation.

[214] Darlan replaced Pierre Laval on December 13, 1940. Darlan came to power with a strong anti-British bias, and was prepared to attack his pre-war ally's African colonies if the Germans allowed it.

[215] Robert Paxton, *Vichy France*, 114.

head of Japy Freres Steel, of which Worms Bank was an important investor. Both men were in key positions to actively collaborate with the occupation forces. On April 29, 1941, Pierre Pucheu, the minister for industrial production, ceded thirty thousand tons of copper to Germany. Jacques Barnaud, the chief economic negotiator for Vichy, signed an agreement on May 8, 1941, with German aluminum interests to double output of this vital commodity.

Gerhard Westrick's brother, Ludger, would have been involved in this negotiation for the German side. In 1941, the bank achieved 24 percent of its profit from German business.[216] Charles Bedaux had used the bank to arrange the transfer of shares and ownership of a client, Blin and Blin, a Jewish-owned textile company, to himself.[217]

The Worms Bank circle was of interest to Dr. Friedrich Grimm, a well-known German international lawyer, who was attached to the staff of Ambassador Abetz. Grimm believed in the transformation of France into a National Socialist state.[218] In a report on his trip to Paris in July-August 1941, he expressed concern over claims that the Worms Group was trying to make the Vichy government more pro-British.[219] These claims were being spread by what he described as leftist circles.

An agent's report described the men of the Worms Group as political-economic pre-war associates interested in putting a fascist leaning government in place.[220] He

---

[216] Philippe Burrin, *France Under the Germans,* 268.

[217] Bedaux used the technique of transfer-of-share ownership for several Jewish-owned French textile enterprises to safeguard them from confiscation by the Nazi occupiers.

[218] Robert Paxton, *Vichy France,* 143.

[219] BAKoblenz, Item 27, 100.

[220] MAFreiburg, RW 5/v 37 F.NR.182 25.7.1941.

describes the Worms men as part of the Darlan government in Vichy, favoring cooperation with Germany, but not closing the door against Britain and the United States. Their attitude, in the final analysis, would be guided by the success of the German military. In other words, they were opportunists. We must remember that this report was written just six weeks after the invasion of the Soviet Union Apparently, everyone was somewhat wary of its outcome.

Worms Bank invested in French Africa and helped financed the expansion of the Ford Motor Company in Oran, Algeria, to build armored vehicles for Erwin Rommel's Afrikacorps in North Africa.[221] Germany's biggest bank, Deutsche Bank, was interested in the Worms Bank leaders' activities. Hermann Abs, a young member of the Deutsche Bank management board, received correspondence from a contact in the occupation administration about Jacques Barnaud's appointment in the Darlan cabinet.[222]

The three largest German banks—Deutsche, Dresdner, and Commerz—competed with one another to get their share of the spoils that came with the Nazi victories.[223] Ziegestar, the first German trustee of Worms Bank, was replaced by Gotthard von Falkenhausen, a Deutsche Bank

---

[221] Hippolyte Worms was arrested for collaboration October 9, 1944, and released in 1948. Jacques Barnaud was arrested October 18, 1944, and released in January 1949; he returned to a management position at the bank and died in 1962. Pierre Pucheau was arrested in Algeria and executed for collaboration with the enemy on March 20, 1944.

[222] Deutsche Bank Archive DBA, ABS 24138. Abs became the bank's chairman in the post-war years.

[223] Commerzbank archive 1/606.

director and a nephew of General von Falkenhausen, the commander of the occupation forces in Belgium.[224]

There was another player who would have participated in the marketing and financing of Bedaux's Africa project, a private German bank well-connected to the Third Reich: Stein Bank in Cologne. It was at the home of its president, Baron Kurt von Schroder, that Hitler and Franz von Papen met in 1933 to make the deal that brought the Nazis to power in Germany. Worms bank was a correspondent of Stein Bank.[225]

Had Bedaux's project moved ahead, France would have issued bonds to finance its developments through a major Paris bank as the lead bank and with Worms and Stein Banks as partners. Individual investors engaged in peanut growing and production along with members of the Worms Group would have been well positioned to take advantage of the investment opportunities.

---

[224] In 2001, Deutsche Bank acquired control of Worms Bank. What a small world this is.

[225] Peter Allen, *The Crown and the Swastika,* 89.

THE ABWEHR

In this chapter we'll examine the record of Charles Bedaux's involvement with German intelligence, limiting our review to the Hitler era, the period from 1933 to 1943. To understand why Bedaux was picked up several times in Gestapo sweeps, we'll also look at how German intelligence was organized. This will not be an in-depth study of the Abwehr, the intelligence arm of the German armed forces under Admiral Wilhelm Canaris, or its dangerous rival for the Führer's attention, the RSHA under Reinhard Heydrich.[226] These organizations and others involved in the Bedaux experience have been discussed in depth elsewhere.[227]

---

[226] Wilhelm Canaris was born on Jan. 1, 1887, and executed on April 9, 1945 (one month before the end of the war), for plotting against Hitler and the Third Reich.

[227] I have used the books *Himmler* by Peter Padfield; *The Game of the Foxes: The Untold Story of German Espionage in the United States and Great Britain During World War II* by Ladislas Farago; *Hitler's Spies: German Military Intelligence in World War II* by David Kahn; and *Canaris* by Heinz Höhne to gain some insight and perspective on the period and the characters involved.

Admiral Wilhelm Canaris took command of the Abwehr in 1935. His intelligence experience dated back to the First World War, when after escaping internment in South America he made his way to Spain, where he was assigned to the intelligence section of the German unit purchasing supplies for the Reich. He was a master at forging ties with the leaders of services of other friendly powers: Spain, Italy, and Hungary. Catholic and pro-monarchist, he had little in common with the Nazi hierarchy, except for the shared fear and hatred of Bolshevism. His department heads were of similar minds, and in the war years became involved in efforts to end the Hitler regime.

As we shall see, Charles Bedaux became a valuable resource for the Abwehr. Indeed, the Abadan project, discussed in an earlier chapter, may well have succeeded if the Abwehr had believed in the ultimate victory of the Third Reich.[228]

Naval officers often have a different worldview from that of their colleagues in the other armed services, as a result of their experience sailing the seven seas. Canaris was an excellent example of this breed, and although his subordinates in key positions in the Abwehr were often army officers, they generally shared his views.[229]

---

[228] Ewald von Kleist-Schmenzin, a conservative anti-Nazi, traveled to London in the summer of 1938 as an emissary of General Ludwig Beck's and Admiral Canaris's in an effort to stop British appeasement of Hitler and to support Czechoslovakia. Von Kleist-Schmenzin was executed April 9, 1945, for participating in the July 20 plot against Hitler.

[229] The Abwehr had eight thousand officers and a total of thirty thousand personnel. (Richard Bassett, *Hitler's Spy Chief*, 167.)

The Abwehr's most dangerous rival in the intelligence operations of the Reich was the *Reichssicherheitshauptamt* (RSHA) under Reinhard Heydrich.[230] The RSHA was responsible for internal security and was part of Heinrich Himmler's Ministry of the Interior. I will spare my readers the gory details of the RSHA's activities. Heydrich, a former low-ranking naval officer who had actually served under Canaris in the 1920s, was in fact the head of intelligence of the Nazi Party. As such, they had unofficial oversight of the Abwehr.

Charles Bedaux was picked up in sweeps by the RSHA during the occupation of France, but released through the intervention of his Abwehr connections.

In 1941, Joachim von Ribbentrop's Ministry of Foreign Affairs, inspired by information it was receiving from diplomats in the Middle East, launched its own intelligence arm, Information III. At its head was Andor Hencke, a career diplomat and Nazi Party member.

The war economy branch, whose chief was General Georg Thomas[231] of the *Oberkommando der Wehrmacht* (OKW), was responsible for analyzing and evaluating economic intelligence. Its staff was almost entirely made up of civilian experts and its mission was to ensure that the armed forces' needs for equipment and weaponry were met. Because of the OKW's expertise in various critical fields, it was used to evaluate the resources available to the Reich's enemies and potential foes.

---

[230] Reinhard Heydrich, born on March 7, 1904, was attacked by an assassin in Prague, where he was deputy protector of Bohemia and Moravia. He died a week later, on June 4, 1942.

[231] Thomas (1890-1946) was involved in planning a military coup against Hitler. He died in Allied custody.

The *Forschungsamt* (F-Amt) under Hermann Göring was responsible for monitoring communications traffic.

There are claims as far back as the First World War that Charles Bedaux was a German agent, when he lived in Grand Rapids, Michigan, and was just starting his consulting business. It certainly was odd that Bedaux would send his wife, young son, and mistress to Japan. Did he have the financial resources at this early stage of his career to finance such a journey? And why Japan? Was his wife being used as a courier, perhaps carrying information about Michigan plants engaged in military production? In 1916 a courier would be required—drawings and plant layouts couldn't be transmitted by technical means. And all travel across the Atlantic was being monitored by the British Navy. This is all speculation, and there is no hard evidence to support it.

As Bedaux's consulting enterprise expanded and went international in the 1920s, his client list brought him into contact with an impressive number of leading world corporations. Information on their activities, capabilities, and resources would certainly have been of interest to intelligence organizations. How and when was he brought to the Third Reich's attention? What we do know is that in 1935, in connection with Bedaux's efforts to continue to operate in Hitler Germany, he came into contact with Emil Georg von Stauss, supervisory board member of Deutsche Bank and Reichstag vice-president, along with Julius Westrick, on assignment by the Büro Ribbentrop in France to foster German-French relations.[232] It would not be a

---

[232] Westrick, a younger brother of Gerhard Alois Westrick, is described as a member of the Nazi colony in Paris during the 1930s. (Roland Ray, *Annaeherung,* 173.)

stretch to believe that Westrick reported back to Berlin upon meeting the wealthy, well-connected French-American.

From May to November 1937, correspondence between Bedaux and von Stauss concerned a new process under development by the Amhempco Company in Danville, Illinois, to produce nitro-cellulose, a product that could be used in explosives. This was at the same time that Bedaux was preparing for the Duke and Duchess of Windsor's trip to Germany. Von Stauss brought the matter to the attention of the Chemical-Technical Reichs Institute of the *Oberkommando des Heeres* (OKH), Germany's High Command of the Army, and the Office for Natural and Synthetic Products of Hermann Göring's Four Year Plan. Before it was over, Vereinigte Glanzstoff and Zellstofffabrik Waldhof, Germany's two leading specialty synthetics companies, were also brought in to evaluate the feasibility of Bedaux's plan. In a letter dated July 10, 1937, Bedaux, who was in Berchtesgaden at the time, told von Stauss that he was eager to meet General Becker, who was in charge of the Chemical-Technical Institute, to discuss explosive production.

In these exchanges, Bedaux expressed his eagerness to be of service, yet there was never any mention of possible compensation.[233] Among the correspondence on the subject is a note from von Stauss, dated September 29, 1937, indicating that *Obergruppenfuhrer* Wilhelm Brueckner, Hitler's chief personal adjutant, stated that Bedaux is very positively evaluated and considered a friend of the Reich. (Brueckner was an early member of the Nazi Party, and had participated in the Beer Hall Putsch with Hitler in Munich

---

[233]   Deutsche Bank archive, von Stauss file.

in 1923.) With this kind of comment, Bedaux must have been most welcome in the upper echelons of the Reich.

The nitro-cellulose process was checked out in detail and included a report from the United States by associates of Zellstofffabrik Waldhof, and it was determined not to be of sufficient interest to warrant further attention.

Bedaux's next encounter with an important Reich official was the meeting with Fritz Wiedemann, Hitler's adjutant, to prepare for the Duke and Duchess of Windsor's visit to Germany in October 1937. Bedaux's role in the Windsor's visit was disastrous for his American image, and he didn't return to America until late 1943, as a prisoner. [234]

Bedaux's view about a dictatorship versus a democracy is best illustrated by a comment made in a speech in Athens in July 1938: "The reason Greece now marches as one man."[235] The ruler of Greece, General Metaxas, had awarded Bedaux an assignment to restructure the country's economy. Bedaux

---

[234] Wiedemann traveled to London to meet with Lord Halifax, the British secretary for foreign affairs, on July 18, 1938. The meeting was arranged by Stephanie von Hohenlohe-Waldenburg-Schillingsfürst (1891-1972), a favorite of Hitler and on the payroll of Lord Rothemere, the owner of the *Daily Mail* and *Daily Mirror* newspapers and one of the richest men in Great Britain. After the Reich's takeover of Austria, von Hohenlohe was awarded the use of Schloss Leopoldskron, a palace confiscated from Max Reinhardt, the famous stage director, where she gave lavish parties, and among her guests was Charles Bedaux. Von Hohenlohe, a half-Jewess from Austria, was Wiedemann's mistress. She followed him to the United States when he was appointed consul-general in San Francisco in 1939. She went on to become the mistress of Major Lemuel Schofield, the head of the U.S. Immigration and Naturalization Service.

[235] *New York Times,* August 1, 1938.

promised that Greece's living standards would rise in only a few years, something that had taken Western democracies fifty years to obtain.

Bedaux continued his relationship with the Windsors, and they became even closer. The contacts we know about led to many meetings, especially when the duke was assigned as the British military liaison to the French army in 1939-1940. During this period, Bedaux, as a citizen of the neutral United States, was able to travel freely to Holland, where his international headquarters were located, and on to Berlin.

The Reich believed that the sympathetic Windsor could change Britain's attitude toward the ambitions of the Reich. In fact, the German embassy in Holland reported several times to Berlin that a group building around the duke was more favorable to a settlement of differences between the Reich and Britain. Bedaux was probably the source of this information.[236]

When Gerhard Westrick became Bedaux's lawyer in 1939, Bedaux was almost immediately brought to the attention of the Abwehr. The German National Archives in Koblenz document the fact that Westrick informed Colonel Brinkmann of the Abwehr about Bedaux's intelligence potential. Westrick also wrote about Bedaux more than once to Dr. Halvor Sudeck, who was probably a member of

---

[236] In the book *Hidden Agenda: How the Duke of Windsor Betrayed the Allies* by Martin Allen, Allen claims that during the so-called phony war period from September 1939 to May 1940, Bedaux acted as Windsor's courier, bringing information to the Nazis in preparation for their attack on the Low Countries and France. To date, there is no conclusive evidence that the duke furnished information that led to a change in the Nazi's offensive plans against France.

the War Economy Branch under General Georg Thomas. This branch collected and evaluated economic information on the Reich's enemies.

Bedaux's circle of contacts within Germany's leadership included an August 23, 1939, visit to Joachim von Ribbentrop, the German foreign Georg von Stauss and Otto Abetz[237] accompanied Bedaux, and it was then that von Ribbontrop advised Bedaux to appoint Westrick as his attorney. Reports concerning Windsor's attitude from the German embassy in Holland during the early months of the war, whose source was very likely Bedaux, would've also been brought to von Ribbentrop's attention. The Ribbentrop ministry organized its own intelligence service in early 1941, when a coup attempt in Iraq was underway.

It is important to note that each of these intelligence services in the Reich were competing for Hitler's attention. The Führer was always skeptical about the intelligence he received, and was believed to have his own independent sources.

Gerhard Westrick, who had served his country in the First World War and had been seriously wounded, badly wanted to serve the Fatherland in the new war. He believed that through his international law connections, he could do this best in the intelligence service. In contact with naval Captain Leopold Bürkner (one of Canaris's closest collaborators and later promoted to vice admiral) and Dr. Halvor Sudeck, Westrick reported on Bedaux's capabilities.

If Bedaux was an agent of long standing, why would the Abwehr be interested in what Westrick had to say about the matter? A logical explanation could be that Bedaux was an

---

[237] In an effort to get approval for the Bedaux company to operate in Germany.

active agent during the First World War, but was dormant during the Weimar Republic. The new regime with Hitler was interested in Bedaux, but the Abwehr was cautious. Could the man be trusted? But there is another possibility, namely that Bedaux, with contacts to Emil Georg von Stauss in the mid-'30s and his arrangements for the Windsors' trip to Germany in 1937, was considered a valuable resource by the Abwehr, and therefore needed cover. Suggestions about Bedaux's potential had to be treated as *Neues* (news, a new source) to ensure that his activities, which had been going on for some time, weren't compromised. Bedaux was very much aware of the support and sympathy Hitler's New World Order had in certain circles in the United States, United Kingdom, and France. He was an excellent candidate for information to the Abwehr.

His consulting companies represented many of the leading American corporations that by this time had expanded internationally. He was in frequent contact with these companies' leaders; Bedaux and Westrick had this in common. The Windsor link was particularly important for Bedaux to establish his bona fides with the new masters of Germany. It's possible that Bedaux may have been one of Hitler's personal sources when we recall that he had rented a villa not far from the Führer's retreat at Berchtesgaden. Bedaux often traveled to Berlin, and would have been able to visit the chancellery unobserved.[238]

Now lets take a look at the facts incriminating Charles Bedaux for collaborating with the enemies of the United States, of which he was a naturalized citizen.

---

[238] This claim is made in *Hidden Agenda* by Martin Allen.

We know from Gerhard Westrick's files[239] that Bedaux was brought to the attention of the Abwehr in 1939. But even before that, Hitler's adjutants, Fritz Wiedemann and Wilhelm Brückner, would have been aware of Bedaux's usefulness. Julius Westrick, the Ribbentrop office representative in Paris in the 1930s, met Bedaux in 1935. Then there was Nikolas (Niko) Bensmann, the Abwehr agent,[240] whose cover was that of an international patent lawyer, and is known to have had contact with Bedaux. All of these would have been "finders" in intelligence parlance, having had recognized Bedaux's usefulness to the Reich. In a letter dated March 2, 1942, Westrick wrote to Dr. Halvor Sudeck (Berlin Halensee, Pauksbornerstr. 83 B), about a recent meeting with Bedaux and the information he received from him concerning activities among the French in North Africa.

Westrick had brought Bedaux to Sudeck's attention almost immediately after his first meeting with his new client. Westrick points out that he received interesting information from Bedaux concerning the personnel close to Marshal Pétain and the French Legion in North Africa. He describes Bedaux as an honest friend of Germany and a fanatic opponent of Bolshevism.[241]

---

[239] BAKoblenz, Bestand 1200, Band 1045. *Nachlass Gerhard Alois Westrick.*

[240] Bensmann, a graduate of Columbia University, had worked in the United States, spoke English fluently, worked for the Texas Oil Company as its German patent lawyer, and was assigned to the Bremen Abwehr station where he was the number-three man. He was considered an expert on the American oil industry and met frequently with Bedaux in Paris.

[241] BAKoblenz, Bestand 1200, Band 1045. *Nachlass Gerhard Alois Westrick.*

In October 1941, Bedaux was invited to Berlin by, some say, Julius Westrick—and perhaps his brother Gerhard was also involved—to discuss his ideas for neutralizing the Abadan refinery in Iran.

I have a copy of his October 30, 1941, debriefing by the Abteilung II, the Abwehr department responsible for special operations and sabotage activities, concerning the situation in French North and West Africa. Colonel Erwin von Lahousen wrote the report's cover letter; von Lahousen headed Abteilung II and was very close to Admiral Canaris, the Abwehr chief.[242]

In von Lahousen's cover letter, Bedaux, who is identified by name, is described as a V-Man, or source-agent, of Abwehr II, and was said to be available for further questioning at the Hotel Adlon in Berlin. The document is a detailed report of Bedaux's trip to Africa starting on August 28, 1941. It described his impressions of the leadership in French North America, including General Maxime Weygand, as well as his conversations with Robert Murphy, President Roosevelt's representative in North Africa. Bedaux also met with Hugh Fullerton, the American consul-general in Marseilles, whom he describes as "pro-German."[243]

The report is noteworthy for Bedaux's evaluation of the personalities with whom he had contact.[244] It also mentions that Bedaux had already reported to Dr. Bensmann about

---

[242] MAFreiburg, Geheime Kommando WI VI/252, dated November 18, 1941.

[243] Murphy had been assigned to the American embassy in Paris in the pre-war years, and was acquainted with Bedaux from this period.

[244] Friends and foes of the New Order are identified, and American plans for possible peaceful intervention in the French colonies is described.

production of agricultural products. With this, we can only conclude that Bedaux had been an Abwehr source for some time.

In his comments Bedaux described Maxime Weygand's attitude in detail as being prepared to deliver the France's African colonies to the British and Americans. These remarks may have led to General Keitel's[245] order to Admiral Canaris to kill Weygand. The order was given orally and then passed on to von Lahousen, who refused to carry it out.[246] [247]

The most incriminating document linking Bedaux to the Third Reich is General von Lahousen's war diary.[248] We know that Bedaux stayed in Berlin to discuss his plans for the Abadan refinery. The entry identifies Charles Bedaux by name and describes him as the designated leader for the planned oil defense action in the Persian Gulf. He described Bedaux as having demanded a number of conditions for his participation, including his entry into the Wehrmacht (armed services), the title of *Kriegsverwaltungschef* (war administration chief), and the rank of *Generalleutnant* (major general).

Because of the conditions on the Eastern Front (the Soviet Union), Admiral Canaris decided to postpone the enterprise, but continued to keep in contact with Bedaux. In

---

[245] Wilhelm Keitel (1882-1946), chief of supreme command of the armed forces, OKW-*Oberkommando der Wehrmacht*. Executed for war crimes after the Nuremberg Trials.

[246] MA 1300-2, p. 436, 445, *Institut für Zeitgeschichte* in Munich.

[247] All United States citizens had been advised to leave France by May 1941. The U.S. bank declined, as did Bedaux's. (RW 49/564#71, Agent R-3748 Paris March 31, 1941.)

[248] Lahousen Diary F23/2A *Institut für Zeitgeschichte* in Munich, dated Dec. 31, 1941.

these discussions about Bedaux's relationship with German intelligence, it's important to note that he was considered to be an agent of the "First Magnitude," an expression used by von Lahousen in his post-war debriefing. As he put it, only the Abwehr's central office handled this category of agent.[249]

Erwin von Lahousen (1897-1959) was one of the few survivors of the unsuccessful plot to eliminate Hitler on July 20, 1944, and was the prosecution's first witness at the major Nuremberg War Crime Trials. Von Lahousen's position as head of Abteilung II of the Abwehr and his close personal relationship with Canaris gave him a unique opportunity to be present at meetings with Hitler and other leading figures of the Third Reich. His comments on Bedaux point to the recognition of the French-American's potential to the Reich. Von Lahousen must be perceived as an honest, trustworthy commentator on events of the Reich.[250]

So the bottom line on Bedaux and German intelligence seems to be that any German who met the man immediately recognized his potential for the Hitler regime. This was true for Emil Georg von Stauss of Deutsche Bank; Julius Westrick of the Ribbentrop staff in Paris in the 1930s; Fritz Wiedemann and Wilhelm Brückner, the Fuehrer's adjutants; Gerhard Westrick, Bedaux's German lawyer; and various German diplomats. There were meetings in Paris in the pre-war years with Nikolas Bensmann of the Abwehr. Were these opportunistic or were they directed? We don't have the answer. What we can say is that if the Abwehr

---

[249]   MA 1300-2, p. 435-445, *Institut für Zeitgeschichte* in Munich.

[250]   Lahousen is given a place of honor in the museum in Vienna dedicated to Austrians who resisted the Third Reich.

leadership had not begun to doubt the direction that Hitler was taking for their beloved Germany, Bedaux's potential would have been better exploited. He was certainly eager to cooperate, but at the same time wanted his backside protected.

HIS CAPTURE AND DEMISE

Hitler's views of the world were colored by his fanatically racist attitude, and they were to lead to fatal errors in his war planning. To Hitler, the Slavic people were only worthy of being slaves to their Aryan masters; therefore, a quick attack against the USSR in June 1941 would lead to an easy conquest. When the United States was attacked at Pearl Harbor on December 7, 1941, Hitler saw only an advantage for the Third Reich in joining the Japanese by declaring war on the Americans on December 11. After all, the United States could manufacture washing machines but not weaponry. Ignoring his own intelligence service, Hitler thought his master race would prevail over them all.

He underestimated his enemies. On November 8, 1942, Allied forces in Operation Torch under the command of General Dwight Eisenhower successfully invaded North Africa, where Charles Bedaux had arrived on October 27 to begin his project to build the peanut oil pipeline and conquer the Sahara. Just prior to the invasion, from September to October 1942, Bedaux and fourteen hundred other

Americans had been interned as a result of a Gestapo sweep, but he was released when the Abwehr intervened.[251] [252]

Bedaux met with Robert Murphy (1894-1978), President Roosevelt's personal representative to French North Africa. The two had first met when Murphy was *charges d'affaires* at the American embassy in Vichy. It was Murphy's assignment to prevent the Vichy commanders in North Africa from resisting the Allied forces and to collect information using the "twelve apostles," twelve young Americans disguised as shipping agents in Algiers, Casablanca, Marrakesh, and Tunis.[253]

Operation Torch was the beginning of the Allies' second front against the Nazis. It was intended to lessen the pressure that the German army poised in front of Stalingrad on the Russian front, and the Afrikacorps of General Rommel advancing from Tunisia on Egypt.

Vichy had over a hundred thousand troops in Algeria, Morocco, and Tunisia, which had initially offered some

---

[251] Along with American women from all over France, Bedaux's wife, Fern, originally from Grand Rapids, Michigan, and her sister Eve, married to Louis S. Duez, were also briefly interned. Fern Bedaux announced to the other women that she would be released quickly, and she and Eve were indeed released after German ambassador Otto Abetz intervened. (Drue Leyton Tartiére, *The House Near Paris*.)

[252] Fern was the youngest of three sisters. Eva was two years older, and Grace was the oldest, four years older. (Grand Rapids [MI] Library archive.) Eva was married to Louis S. Duez, the owner of a consulting company in which Charles Bedaux was briefly employed in 1913.

[253] Murphy was honored with other diplomats in a stamp series issued by the United States Postal Service in 2006.

resistance to the Allied forces.[254] The Vichy commander was General Weygand, who had been commanding general when the Germans invaded France in June 1940.

The French, under the command of Admiral Jean-Francois Darlan, agreed to a cease-fire, and surrendered on November 11. General Eisenhower agreed to recognize the Vichyite Darlan as the political head of French North Africa, which unleashed a major controversy with General Charles de Gaulle's Free French Forces.[255]

Among a small group of French men who operated with Murphy to prepare for Operation Torch was Jacques Lemaigre Dubreuil, the director of France's largest vegetable oil producer, Lesieur, which had vast holdings of peanut plantations on the Niger River, the end goal of Bedaux's Sahara pipeline scheme. Lemaigre Dubreuil was suspected of leaking information in advance of Operation Torch so that he and certain French bankers could make a "killing on currency fluctuations after the invasion."[256] [257]

---

[254] The Allied forces suffered 663 deaths. (Robert Paxton, *Vichy France.*)

[255] Darlan was assassinated on December 24, 1942, and replaced by General Henri Giraud, who had escaped from captivity in Germany.

[256] John H. Waller, *The Unseen War in Europe*, 261.

[257] In late March 1943, the Giraud government in Algiers dismissed Lemaigre Dubreuil, "who had taken a devious but potent hand in North African affairs." He had been an inter-allied economic advisor in Algiers. French speculators had transferred millions of francs when the exchange was 100-150 francs to the dollar. On French advice the rate was changed to 50 francs on the dollar. Speculators made a profit of 100 percent and more. (*Time* magazine, April 3, 1943).

Bedaux, who had no qualms about showing his special passes to Murphy—one from Laval and the other (the Ausweis) from the Nazi occupiers—stayed at the Hotel Aletti. The official start of Bedaux's mission was to be November 15, 1942. Soon after his arrival, Bedaux had a number of meetings with the engineers on his team.

On November 7, Bedaux had to vacate his suite at the hotel to make room for a German general. He moved in with Captain Fritz Wormann of the Wehrmacht, an Abwehr officer who was probably assigned to monitor the French-American. Bedaux and his German roommate spent the morning of November 8 sitting on the terrace of their suite drinking brandy and observing the action as the Allied forces invaded.

Bedaux was finally arrested by the French on December 5 and held until December 29. In the weeks before this, he was a frequent guest of parties hosted by French ladies, which senior officers of the Allies also attended. On January 2, 1943, he was rearrested by the French at the United States' request and kept for eleven months in a military barracks in El Biar, a suburb of Algiers.[258] [259]

Whenever Bedaux traveled on an extended trip, he did so accompanied by what was tantamount to a file cabinet of correspondence, records, photos, and various papers. These were, of course, kept in expensive, custom-made luggage.

---

[258] Bedaux's arrest was covered in a front-page story in the *New York Times* on January 14, 1943.

[259] The French had enough evidence to execute Bedaux but he claimed United States citizenship, so France's agreement with the Americans left it to the United States to decide his fate. (John McVane, in a letter published in the November 3, 1945, *New Yorker*. McVane was a radio news correspondent in North Africa.)

This time, a detailed questionnaire in French regarding the Allied military disposition was included. Was this planted among Bedaux's documents during the period of December 5-29, when he was under French control? Did it get in among his papers through some clerical error when the French examined his papers? Why didn't he destroy this incriminating document? All these are unanswered questions that could prove without a shadow of a doubt that he was an espionage agent.

The "files" included photos of the Duke and Duchess of Windsor at Chateau de Candé, but did not include correspondence with the former king. There were British intelligence operators in the area, of course, who may have had access to Bedaux's papers while he was under French control. There would have been considerable interest in neutralizing any possible incriminating or embarrassing correspondence between the royal duke and his wily French-American friend.[260]

Two FBI agents, assistant director Percy E. Foxworth and special agent Harold Haberfield, were dispatched to interrogate Bedaux. But they died on January 15, 1943, when their aircraft crashed in South America while en route to North Africa. Foxworth was considered the FBI's most experienced counter-espionage specialist, having captured a number of German agents. Two other FBI men followed,

---

[260]   Charles Bedaux's son, Charles Emile Bedaux (1909-1993), was in North Africa as a member of the team that was to work on the pipeline project. He was temporarily put under arrest with his father, but was released when he was acknowledged to be an American citizen by birth. He served in the United States Army.

and they completed their interrogation in early spring of 1943.[261]

The Germans wanted Bedaux released. A German official, Dr. Keller, was contacted in November 1943 by Andre Envere—a friend and associate of Édouard Herriot, a former premier of France who was under control of the Nazis—about improving Herriot's living conditions. Keller offered a deal if Bedaux could be exchanged. René de Chambrun, an international lawyer, descendant of Lafayette and son-in-law of Pierre Laval, also tried to negotiate Bedaux's release.[262]

The British were provided details of Bedaux's interrogation. Guy Liddell, director of counter espionage, wrote this in his war diary on November 29, 1943: "Isos and Harlequin show that he has told only the half-truth interspersed with a few lies." Isos was the British decrypts operation and Harlequin was a high-level German defector in North Africa. Bedaux described his visit to Berlin in October 1941 as having been cleared by Elto Elkington of

---

[261] The Justice Department requested that Lloyd Cutler, a twenty-six-year-old lawyer on assignment with the North Africa Economic Board, liaison with the two FBI men. After the war, Cutler became a prominent lawyer in Washington, DC, and served as special counsel in the Carter and Clinton administrations. He died in 2005 at the age of eighty-seven.

[262] Édouard Herriot, born in 1872, a schoolteacher and politician, was appointed to the cabinet during the first world war. In 1924, he was given the title of premier in a coalition government of radicals and socialists. He was president of the Chamber of Deputies in 1940, and initially supported Pétain as the Vichy leader. Herriot was arrested by the Vichy police in 1942, turned over to the Nazis, and deported to Germany in 1944. He survived the war, and went on to play a minor role in post-war politics.

the Anglo-Iranian Oil Company. When the British checked with Elkington, he denied having anything to do with Bedaux's visit to Berlin. "Bensmann was in Berlin for the Bedaux meeting and ordered to introduce Bedaux to Dr. Endrou."[263]

Bedaux was finally returned to the United States. He arrived in Miami on December 23, 1943, the closest point of entry for air traffic from Africa, and was put under the control of the Immigration and Naturalization Service. The first thing that had to be established was whether Bedaux was still a citizen of the United States. He had not been in the United States since late 1937, when he was confronted by his American staff, the press, and labor unions for his Nazi connections and for arranging the Windsors' visit to the Third Reich. Edward J. Ennis, administrator of Foreign Travel Control in the Department of Justice, was responsible for investigating Bedaux's citizenship, and he assigned it to his assistant, John L. Burling.

Under U.S. law at the time, a naturalized citizen who returned to his country of origin for residence for two or more years was presumed to have lost his American citizenship. Bedaux was now in a quandary, between a rock and a hard place. If it were decided that he was French, he would have been returned to Algeria, where the Free French Forces might have executed him. If it were decided that he was an American citizen, he could have been charged with treason. United States law dating from the founding of the republic stated that the proof of treason required two witnesses to verify the charge.

On December 28, Burling began the hearing to decide whether Bedaux was a U.S. citizen, and the hearing

---

[263] Nigel West, *Guy Liddell Diaries, Vol. II*, 143.

went through December 31. His passport had expired on February 27, 1942, but that didn't cause him to lose citizenship. He was asked why he had not left France when he had the chance, and why—when leaving France was no longer possible—he hadn't attempted to escape, as others had done. He had an answer for every question except the last.[264]

Bedaux was straightforward in answering questions about his relations with the Germans, and candid about his ideas and his person. He made four points in his defense: 1) he had saved lives, 2) he had helped release one hundred Jews from concentration camps and helped release American citizens from internment in Compiègne, 3) he had been friendly with the Nazis to get their plans, and 4) he had used his Nazi contacts to gain control of Bedaux International in Holland so he could pay the tax money due to the American government.[265] As always, he was glib and fascinating, and charmed his interrogators with his French accent and extreme self-confidence. Throughout the hearing he claimed to be an American citizen.

Six weeks after the hearing ended, Bedaux learned that Burling and Ennis had been appointed special criminal division assistants to the attorney general, and that they were to seek a grand jury indictment of Bedaux for treason and communicating with the enemy. On Valentine's Day 1944 he was informed that he was indeed still a United States citizen, and that he would be charged with treason.

---

[264] Janet Flanner, *New Yorker* article.
[265] Ibid.

But this would have been very difficult to prove. Where were the two witnesses?[266]

But there was a second charge, first used in the Civil War, of communicating with the enemy, and the peanut oil project would have provided the evidence. He met with his lawyer, Edmund I. Jones, and that night Bedaux committed suicide. He overdosed on Luminal, the sleeping pill to which he was addicted, and was rushed to Jackson Memorial Hospital in Miami. He died on February 18, 1944.

His death made front-page news in the United States, including the *New York Times* and the *Miami Herald*, and in the controlled press of occupied Paris. He was described as a true friend of Europe's New Order and a "convinced partisan of collaboration with Greater Germany."[267] In occupied France, the press described him as an "honest man who was a convinced partisan of collaboration with Greater Germany."[268] Wild speculation about his death followed, such as that his death had been ordered so he couldn't testify to the fascist leanings of some prominent Americans. This speculation was highly unlikely in light of the fact that Fern Bedaux, his American wife, was still in occupied France,

---

[266] There were a number of reports about Bedaux's activities during the German occupation. One of the most devastating was that of Herman and Katherine Rogers, who were friends of the Windsors. In August 1941 in Lisbon while en route to the United States, they denounced Bedaux as a collaborator with the Nazis to an American diplomat. (Charles Glass, *Americans in Paris*, 200.)

[267] Janet Flannery, *New Yorker* article.

[268] Ibid.

and his love for her would have precluded anything that would possibly have put her in harm's way.[269]

Was this the end of the Bedaux story? No. In October 1944, the French government, which now operated in liberated Paris, awarded Charles Bedaux his third *Légion d'honneur* for his economic contribution to the well-being of France.[270] Tours now has a Charles Bedaux Avenue. Today we wonder, why honor the man who was, at a minimum, a collaborator with the Nazi occupiers? Was it another example of France demonstrating its independence from its American liberator? In October 1944, of course, they couldn't have known of von Lahousen's December 1941 diary entry in which Bedaux listed his terms for embracing the Reich's cause. The claim that they examined the facts and found Bedaux innocent is strange.

Then there was Britain's attitude toward the Bedaux-Windsor relationship. The links between the French-American consultant and the former King Edward VIII were much closer than has often been recognized or admitted. It's understandable that the royal family would want to avoid further embarrassment. We know that Bedaux always traveled with files of correspondence of all sorts. During his captivity in Algiers in December 1942 and before his departure to the United States, British operatives

---

[269] At this stage, the attorney general was in charge of the case. At some point, however, the Bedaux affair would have been brought to President Roosevelt's attention—and in the case of eight German saboteurs, Roosevelt had insisted that they be tried by a military tribunal. They were, and six were executed.

[270] In 1961 he received a fourth *Légion d'honneur* for his contribution to the rebuilding of Tours during the war.

could have cleaned Bedaux's papers of any incriminating notes or correspondence related to the royal duke.

What we do know about Britain's sensitivity regarding the Duke of Windsor is a result of the situation involving Anthony Blunt (1907-1983). Blunt, a graduate of Cambridge who was later put in charge of the royal family's art collection, was a member of British intelligence. He was also a Soviet agent in the 1930s, '40s, and '50s. In 1945, he was assigned to recover correspondence between Queen Victoria and her daughter, who was the wife of Kaiser Friedrich Wilhelm.

Was this truly Blunt's mission? Or was it to recover correspondence between the Prince of Hesse and the Duke of Windsor and Bedaux? All three communicated with one another. The site for what turned out to be a *Nacht und Nebel* (Night and Fog) operation was Kronberg Castle, not far from Frankfurt. The date was the summer of 1945, a short time after the Second World War ended in May 1945. Denied entrance to the attic, where such correspondence was suspected to be stored, Blunt managed to gain access. What he recovered remains a mystery to this day, and the stated reason for the mystery was entirely logical. Queen Victoria and her daughter, the empress widow of Kaiser Friedrich, did have an extensive correspondence. The Prince of Hesse, however, who often sympathized with the Nazi cause, had resided in the castle in the 1930s and '40s, and corresponded with the duke and, possibly, Bedaux.[271]

---

[271] Kronberg castle was remodeled after being requisitioned by the Americans into a five-star hotel. In January 1954, a nine-hole golf course club was founded on its grounds by a group led by Wolfgang Prinz von Hessen, and included Gerhard Westrick, Bedaux's lawyer. I became a member of this club in 1962. Oh, what a small world this is.

Once, in a speech to a group of American businessmen, Bedaux said, "A man loves his country. He makes laws for the glory of his flag. He traces the outline of a national ideal he would like to live up to, but in his stomach, his needs for trade are essentially international. He is a patriot, and a sincere one, but when his money is concerned, he blissfully commits treason." Bedaux thought so highly of this comment that he had it copyrighted.

What was it that brought Bedaux to throw his lot in with the rulers of the Third Reich? Bedaux's business experience was consulting others on how to make their production more efficient by making labor more productive. With his plan to conquer the Sahara, he would show the world that he could create one of the wonders of the century. Perhaps it was the need for recognition and the power it represented that drove him.

Bedaux was buried in a cemetery in Boston, "almost in the shadow of the tomb of Mary Baker Eddy, founder of the Christian Science Church."[272] Bedaux's estate was left in trust for his wife, Fern. In a will drawn on April 22, 1926, upon her death, his son was to receive twenty thousand dollars per year, and his nieces and nephews were each to receive two thousand dollars per year.[273]

There were all sorts of wild rumors that appeared after Bedaux's death. Among them was that some pro-Nazi American industrialists had organized his end to ensure that he would not testify against them. The more likely explanation for Bedaux's suicide was to avoid the embarrassment of being tried in an American court for collaboration with a United States enemy, and probably to

---

[272] Article in the *New York Times,* February 23, 1944.

[273] Article in the *New York Times*, June 15, 1944.

protect his wife Fern, who remained in occupied France. Some would say she was a kind of hostage to ensure Bedaux's cooperation in the Sahara project. Bedaux's good friend, General Franz Albrecht Medicus, the co-author of the infamous, anti-Semitic Nuremberg Laws of 1935, and a leading official in the occupation, had assured Bedaux that Fern would always be under his protection. And so she was. Fern employed Franz Albrecht Medicus's daughter after the war. Fern continued to reside in Chateau de Candé, made an effort to carry on the Bedaux consultancies with little success, and died in 1972.[274]

---

[274] In 2005, a painting of Fern in a Japanesque robe that was painted in 1925 by Nicolas Becker was offered at an auction in Paris. Fern had given the chateau to the French government in 1951. Upon her death, the government turned the chateau over to Conseil Général d'Indre-et-Loire.

UNANSWERED QUESTIONS

For me, this has been a long journey, approaching twelve years as we reach the final stage. It was not, however, an effort in futility. On the contrary . . . it has been a tremendous learning experience.

Charles Eugène Bedaux has been described as an enigma, and in many respects he was. He was comparable to the fast-talking medicine men at the turn of the nineteenth century. His system would solve everyone's management and labor problems.

His renowned system to increase worker productivity through an incentive system was clever, but it also discouraged management from investing in plants and equipment. Increased short-term profits were a strong selling proposition for those adopting Bedaux's approach.

His successful consulting business—and it was huge—led to great wealth and power. The power came from contacts with men in high places, an unreal experience for the uneducated but intelligent French-American. What we can say is, only in America was such an achievement possible. Had he not been hired as an interpreter by the Italian engineer A. M. Morrini, who was studying American production methods, his life would probably have taken an entirely different path.

What was Bedaux, on balance? What were the pros and cons on which to assess or judge the man? He made a fortune, married well in his second marriage, which eased his way into contacts at the upper levels of society. The Bedauxs were listed in the Social Register of New York society.

What was particularly noteworthy about the man is that he was curious and eager to learn. His travels in Africa and elsewhere were not the typical jaunts of the well to do. He traveled in first-class style, but always with a mission to learn what could be best applied to his business. He was also developing the talents of the ideal intelligence operator. But, was he or wasn't he? Some would say he was an idealist, misunderstood but honorable. I come away with another verdict.

Bedaux, physically small but with an overpowering personality, had become enchanted with the Third Reich, or, as he saw it, the New Order in a chaotic world. Of course he was not alone. Others among the leading personalities of the West, such as Colonel Charles Lindbergh and Henry Ford, saw the Reich as a savior against communism.

Then there was Edward, the Duke of Windsor, who abdicated the throne for the love of a twice-divorced American, Mrs. Simpson. Edward and Mrs. Simpson married at Chateau de Candé, Bedaux's home, and the two men became friends. The friendship would only enhance the Reich's interest in the French-American.

When did Bedaux's contacts with German intelligence begin? As the files indicate, he certainly came under suspicion by United States security during the First World War, while living in Grand Rapids. If he had been in German service at the time, there was no recognition or connection with the apparatus of the Third Reich. But in the years of Nazi Germany's attempt to conquer Europe, there is no question that Charles Bedaux became an eager agent of the Abwehr. In 1935, Bedaux, anxious to get his German company back into the fold, met with Emil Georg von Stauss of Deutsche Bank and Julius Westrick, the Ribbentrop office representative in France. One of Westrick's assignments was to identify friends of the Reich. He would certainly have reported to von Ribbentrop, whose office was the Nazi's foreign affairs watchdog.

Gerhard Westrick, the renowned international lawyer, spotted Bedaux's potential value for the Reich when they met in 1939. There is evidence in the national archive in Koblenz that Westrick contacted high-level officers of the Abwehr on the matter.

For me, it has been a question of connecting the dots, and I hope that readers will believe that I have had some measure of success.[275]

The big unanswered question is why did an extremely successful self-made man, who made his wealth in the United States democracy, become an agent of the Third Reich? What tipped the scale?

In October 1937 he left the United States, having been forced to renounce control of his American company due to the negative press in connection with the Windsor visit to Hitler Germany, which he had arranged. This was a terrible blow to his pride. An immigrant who had achieved a fortune and whose name was in the Social Register had to

---

[275] I wasn't able to access the Soviet Russian archive on Bedaux, which undoubtedly has interesting information.

experience this public embarrassment; it must have been a tough nut to swallow.

His achievements and his wealth brought new friends and new opportunities. Who could imagine that an ex-king of a world empire would choose to marry at Bedaux's chateau and become a friend of the French-American? This was a fact that only increased his value as an asset of German intelligence.

With the wave of the future, fascism and the National Socialist German Workers Party, the Bedaux System could solve the world's problems.

For Bedaux, the occupation of France demonstrated the "decadence" of his native land and the strength of the Nazi rulers. He became a friend of General Franz Albrecht Medicus, an important figure in the occupation, who in 1935 had co-authored the infamous anti-Jewish Nuremberg Laws.

We can imagine Bedaux's joy in 1941 when Marshal Pétain agreed to let him demonstrate the his idealistic "equivilism" plan by putting the Roquefort area at his disposal. Equivilism was Bedaux's utopian idea for the world in which money was to be replaced by a new unit of human energy called the B. As Bedaux described it, his idea would put "capitalism into communism."

This was not his first attempt to demonstrate equivilism's feasibility. Just prior to the start of the war, Bedaux had signed an agreement with the Greek government to reorganize Greece's economy on the basis of the Bedaux System. But the assignment was never implemented because of the war. So, was Bedaux an idealist, a utopian, or was there something else in the man's character to explain his actions? With all of these achievements, the French-American soon believed that he could do almost anything. Why not put a former king back on the throne of the British Empire, as some in the Reich believed possible?

The thought had to be exhilarating for a man like Bedaux, who had come from nowhere and achieved so much.

Bedaux made no secret of his activities with the Germans. He drove around Paris with special license plates awarded only to collaborators of the occupied regime. He told American officials about some of his assignments. Bedaux probably believed he was above the law, and all would end well with some kind of negotiated peace. He was not alone with these ideas.

Another unsolved mystery about Charles Bedaux is the two posthumous Légion d'honneur awards by the French government, which added to the two he had received in 1936 and 1940. They were awarded in October 1944, shortly after the liberation of Paris by the Allies, and in 1960. The latter was for his assistance to the city of Tours during the occupation. In fact, there is an Avenue Charles Bedaux in Tours, France. What could have motivated France to overlook or ignore the fact that Bedaux had been charged with collaborating with the Nazis?[276]

Bedaux had once said of his work with the Germans, "They were the only ones you could do business with." Many French collaborators had the same attitude, and quite a few served in high government office and business in the years after the war.

In many ways, Charles Bedaux envisioned himself as a savior. Mankind, so his thinking may well have been, needed

---

[276] He had received his second *Légion d'honneur* in 1940, although British intelligence had warned their French counterpart about doing business with Bedaux.

a Hitler to organize politically, and a Bedaux to do the same for the world's economy. His idea for developing the peanut economy was not far-fetched: the hungry in Africa are now being kept alive by a product called Plumpy'nut, which is five hundred calories of fortified peanut butter.

At another time and under other circumstances, Bedaux's plans for developing the Sahara Desert may well have led to the recognition as a savior that he so desired. On the question of the importance of Bedaux's contribution to scientific management, I will not attempt to evaluate it; rather, I will leave it to others more qualified than I. There is, however, no doubt that through the rapid expansion of his international operations, Bedaux made business consulting an important tool. Many new consulting enterprises were spawned from Bedaux's operations.

Let's leave well enough alone with the city of Tour's recognition, complete with an Avenue Charles Bedaux. I hope that Grand Rapids, Michigan, the birthplace of Bedaux's consulting business, will refrain from doing the same.

BIBLIOGRAPHY

Allen, Martin. *Hidden Agenda: How the Duke of Windsor Betrayed the Allies.* London: M. Evans and Co., 2002.

Allen, Peter. *The Crown and the Swastika.* London: R. Hale, 1983.

Andrew, Christopher. *The Sword and the Shield.* New York: Basic Books, 1999.

Bassett, Richard. *Hitler's Spy Chief: The William Canaris Mystery.* London: Cassell, 2005.

Bryan, J. III and Murphy, Charles J. V. *The Windsor Story: An Intimate Portrait of Edward VIII and Mrs. Simpson.* New York: Morrow, 1979.

Bundesarchiv Koblenz, Bestand 1200, Band 1045. *Nachlass Gerhard Alois Westrick.*

Bundesarchiv-Militärarchiv, Freiburg

Burrin, Philippe. *France Under the Germans.* New York: The New Press, 1996.

Carney, Colwell. Memorandum.

Christy, Jim. *The Price of Power: A Biography of Charles Eugène Bedaux.* New York: Doubleday, 1984.

Cogan, Charles G. *Oldest Allies, Guarded Friends.* Westport: Praeger, 1994.

Coignard, S. & Guichard, M.T. *French Connections, Networks and Influence*. New York: Algora Publishing, 2000.

Cole, Hubert. *Laval*. New York: G. P. Putnam & Sons, 1963.

Crockett, Richard. *Twilight of the Truth*. New York: St. Martin's Press, 1989.

Curtis, Michael. *Verdict on Vichy*. New York: Arcade, 2002.

Deutsche Bank Archive. *Von Stauss File, Vol. 4*. Berlin.

Dobran, Michael. *Off Road Sub Arctic Odyssey: Mysterious Adventure of M. Charles Bedaux*.1994.

Donaldson, Francis. *Edward VIII*. New York: Lippincott, 1975.

Erkner, Paul. *Zeitschrift für Unternehmensgeschichte*, 41, no. 2 (1998): 139-158.

Farrago, Ladislas. *The Game of the Foxes: The Untold Story of German Espionage in the United States*. New York: McRay, 1971.

Flanner, Janet. "Department of Amplification: Annals of Collaboration," *New Yorker*, three-part article: Sept. 22, Oct. 6 and Oct. 13, 1945.

Franz, Corinna. *Fernand de Brinon und die Deutsch-Französischen Beziehungen 1918-1945*. Bonn: Bouvier Verlag, 2000.

Friedlander, Saul. *Nazi Germany and the Jews. Vol. 1*. New York: HarperCollins, 1997.

Gall, Lothar. *The Deutsche Bank 1870-1995*. London: Weidenfeld & Nicolson, 1995.

Glass, Charles. *Americans in Paris: Life and Death Under Nazi Occupation*. New York: The Penguin Press, 2010.

Hardwick, Cyril. *Time Study in Treason: Charles E. Bedaux—Patriot or Collaborator?* Chelmsford: "Skylark" Pleshey, 1990.

Hayes, Peter. *Industry and Ideology.* New York: Cambridge University Press, 2001.

Higham, Charles. *American Swastika.* New York: Doubleday, 1985.

Higham, Charles. *The Duchess of Windsor: The Secret Life.* Hoboken: Wiley, 2005.

Higham, Charles. *Trading with the Enemy.* New York: Delacorte Press, 1983.

Hildebrand, Klaus. *Vom Reich zum Weltreich: Hitler, NSDAP und Koloniale Frage 1919-1945.* Munich: Fink, 1969.

Hildebrand, Klaus. *The Foreign Policy of the Third Reich.* Berkeley: University of California Press, 1973.

Höhne, Heinz. *Canaris.* New York: Cooper Square Press, 1979.

Hoisington Jr., William H. *A Businessman in Politics in France: The Career of Jacques Lemaigre Dubreuil 1935-1955.* PhD diss., Stanford University, 1968.

Hughes, Thomas P. *American Genesis: A Century of Invention and Technological Enthusiasm, 1870-1970.* Chicago: University of Chicago Press, 2004.

Hyde, H. Montgomery. *The Quiet Canadian.* London: Hamish Hamilton, 1962.

Ind, Allison. *A History of Modern Espionage.* London: Hodder & Stoughton, 1965.

Institut für Zeitgeschichte, Munich, von Lahousen War Diary

James, Harold. *Deutsche Bank and the Nazi Economic War Against the Jews.* New York: Cambridge University Press, 2001.

James, Harold. *The Nazi Dictatorship and the Deutsche Bank.* New York: Cambridge University Press, 2004.

James, Harold. *Verbandspolitik Im Dritten Reich.* Munich: Piper, 2001.

Janssen, Gregor. *Das Ministerium Speer*. Frankfurt: Ullstein, 1968.

Jones, David Bryce. *Paris in the Third Reich*. New York: Holt, Rinehart & Winston, 1981.

Jorgensen, Christer. *Hitler's Espionage Machine*. Guilford: Lyons Press, 2004.

Kahn, David. *Hitler's Spies: German Military Intelligence in World War II*. New York: Da Capo Press, 1978.

Kaplan, Alice. *The Collaborator*. Chicago: University of Chicago Press, 2000.

Kempner, Robert. *Ankläger Einer Epoche*. Berlin: Ullstein, 1986.

Kipping, Matthias. "American Management Consulting Companies in Western Europe, 1920 to 1990: Products, Reputation, and Relationships." *The Business History Review*, 73, no. 2 (Summer 1999): 190-220.

Kitchen, Martin. *A Military History of Germany*. London: Weidenfeld & Nicholson, 1975.

Koch, Peter Ferdinand. *Die Geldgeschäfte der SS*. Hamburg: Hoffman & Campe, 2000.

Laquer, Walter. *Fascism Past, Present, Future*. New York: Oxford University Press, 1996.

Leveaux, Yves & Nikitin, Marc. *From Workshop to Utopia. Two Consultants and Their Projects for Society in Turmoil (1917-1962)*. 2005. Manuscript via Google.

Leverkühn, Paul. *German Military Intelligence*. New York: Praeger, 1954.

Linne, Karsten. 1996. "*Ein Amerikanischer Geschäftsmann Und Die Nationalsozialisten: Charles Bedaux.*" *Zeitschrift fuer Geschichtswissenschaft*, 44, no. 9: 809.

Lottman, Herbert. *Pétain: Hero or Traitor?* New York: Morrow, 1985.

Lottman, Herbert R. *The Purge, Purification of French Collaborators After World War II.* New York: Morrow, 1986.

Martin, James Steward. *All Honorable Men.* Boston: Little Brown, 1950.

Memoir of George Stauss—Part II. Five Years in Europe—October 1934-1939. 1950. Manuscript via Google.

Nossiter, Adam. *Algeria Hotel.* New York: Houghton Mifflin, 2001.

Oursler Jr., Fulton. "Secret Treason," *American Heritage Magazine.* December 1991.

Ousby, Ian. *Occupation.* New York: St. Martin's Press, 1998.

Padfield, Peter. *Himmler.* New York: MIF Books, 1990.

Paxton, Robert. *Vichy France: Old Guard and New Order 1940-1944.* New York: Columbia University Press, 1982.

Penrose, Barrie & Freeman, Simon. *Conspiracy of Silence.* New York: Vintage,1988.

Persico, Joseph. *Roosevelt's Secret War.* New York: Random House, 2001.

Petropoulos, Jonathon. *Royals and the Reich.* New York: Oxford University Press, 2006.

Pohl, Manfred. *VIAG.* Munich: Piper, 1998.

Pool, James. 1997. *Hitler And His Secret Partners.* New York: Pocket Books, 1997.

Pool, James. 1997. *Who Financed Hitler.* New York: Pocket Books, 1997.

Ray, Roland. 2000. *Annäherung an Frankreich im Dienste Hitler's?* Munich: Oldenbourg, 2000.

"Rheinisch-Westfälisches Wirtschaftsarchiv zu Köln." Die Geschichte Der Unternehmerischen Selbstverwaltung

in Köln 1914-1997. Köln: Rheinisch-Westfälisches Wirtschaftsarchiv, 1997.

Schad, Martha. *Hitler's Spy Princess.* Gloucestershire: Sutton Publishing, 2004.

Schwanitz, Wolfgang. *Germany and the Middle East, 1871-1945.* Princeton: Markus Wiener, 2004.

Schweitzer, Arthur. *Big Business in the Third Reich.* London: Eyre & Spottiswoode, 1964.

Sereny, Gitta. *Albert Speer, His Battle with Truth.* New York: Vintage Books, 1995.

Shields, J. G. "Charlemagne's Crusaders: French Collaboration in Arms, 1941-1945," *French Cultural Studies* 18 (February 2007): 83-105.

Shirer, William. *The Rise and Fall of the Third Reich.* New York: Simon & Schuster, 1960.

Smith, Page. *America Enters the World.* New York: McGraw Hill, 1985.

Speer, Albert. *Inside the Third Reich: Memoirs.* New York: Simon & Schuster, 1970.

Sprecher, Drexel. *Inside the Nuremberg Trials.* Lawham: University Press of America, 1999.

Steinberg, Jonathan. *The Deutsche Bank and Its Gold Transactions During the Second World War.* Munich: C. S. Beck, 1999.

Tartiére, Drue. *The House Near Paris: An American Woman's Story of Traffic in Patriots.* New York: Simon & Schuster, 1946.

Taylor, Edmond. *Awakening from History.* Boston: Gambit, 1969.

Time magazine.

Thomas, Gwynne. *King, Pawn or Black Knight.* London: Mainstream Publishing, 1995.

Thorpe, Andrew. *The British Communist Party and Moscow 1920-1943*. New York: Manchester University Press, 2000.

Vassiltchikov, Marie. *Berlin Diaries 1940-1945*. New York: Vintage Books, 1988.

Vinen, Richard. *The Politics of French Business 1936-1945*. New York: Cambridge University Press, 1991.

Walker, John H. *The Unseen War in Europe*. New York: Random House, 1996.

Weber, Eugene. *The Hollow Years*. New York: Norton, 1994.

Weighton, Charles & Peis, Gunter. *They Spied on England*. London: Odhams Press, 1958.

Weitz, John. *Hitler's Banker*. New York: Little Brown & Co., 1987.

West, Nigel. *Guy Liddell Diaries, Vol. I & II 1942-1945*. London: Routledge, 2005.

Westrich, Robert. *Who's Who in Nazi Germany*. New York: Macmillan, 1982.

Wheelock, John Hall. *The Last Romantic: A Poet Among Publishers: The Oral Autobiography of John Hall Wheelock*. Columbia: University of South Carolina Press, 2002.

Winterbotham, F.W. *The Nazi Connection*. New York: Harper & Row, 1978.